VIRTUES

YOUR CHRISTIAN LEGACY

VIRTUES

YOUR CHRISTIAN LEGACY

SUSAN MUTO

EMMAUS
ROAD
PUBLISHING

STEUBENVILLE, OHIO
A DIVISION OF CATHOLICS UNITED FOR THE FAITH
WWW.EMMAUSROAD.ORG

Emmaus Road Publishing
827 North Fourth Street
Steubenville, Ohio 43952

Library of Congress Control Number: 2014937457
ISBN: 978-1-940329-81-9

The Revised Standard Version of the Bible: Second Catholic Edition
was published in 2006 with ecclesiastical approval of the
United States Conference of Catholic Bishops.

Cover design & layout by: Theresa Westling

Books by Susan Muto, PhD

Approaching the Sacred: An Introduction to Spiritual Reading
Blessings That Make Us Be: A Formative Approach to Living the Beatitudes
Caring for the Caregiver
Catholic Spirituality A to Z: An Inspirational Dictionary
Celebrating the Single Life: A Spirituality for Single Persons in
Today's World
Dear Master: Correspondence on Spiritual Direction Inspired by
St. John of the Cross
Deep Into the Thicket: Soul Searching Meditations Inspired by
The Spiritual Canticle of St. John of the Cross
John of the Cross for Today: The Ascent
John of the Cross for Today: The Dark Night
The Journey Homeward: On the Road of Spiritual Reading
Keepsakes for the Journey
Late Have I Loved Thee: The Recovery of Intimacy
Meditation in Motion
One in the Lord: Living the Call to Christian Community
Pathways of Spiritual Living
A Practical Guide to Spiritual Reading
Practicing the Prayer of Presence
Praying the Lord's Prayer with Mary
Renewed at Each Awakening
Steps Along the Way: The Path of Spiritual Reading
Table of Plenty: Good Food for Body and Soul
Where Lovers Meet: Inside the Interior Castle
Womanspirit: Reclaiming the Deep Feminine in our Human Spirituality
Words of Wisdom for Our World:
The Precautions and Counsels of St. John of the Cross

TABLE OF CONTENTS

PART FOUR – VIRTUES OF THE GLOBAL LIFE

The spiritual virtues must be nurtured and
all the rest made subject to them.
—St. Francis de Sales

[T]est everything; hold
fast what is good,
abstain from every form of evil.
(1 Thessalonians 5:21–22)

5

INTRODUCTION

Scan the headlines. Watch the news on television. Go to an action movie. Quickly we conclude that vice triumphs over virtue. Forgotten or neglected is the legacy left to us by good parents and teachers, by spiritual writers and saints, who are as inspiring to us today as they were to believers and sincere seekers in the past. Think of how many times the Golden Rule has been broken because we do not do unto others what we would have them do for us.

To correct this lack of attention to virtuous living in all facets of our life is the aim of this book. The theological virtues of faith, hope, and love, like the cardinal virtues of prudence, justice, fortitude, and temperance, are empowering gifts of God. Scripture offers many passages devoted to excelling in the virtues. Here are some exemplary descriptions offered by the Apostle Paul:

> Therefore, since we are justified by faith, we have peace with God through our Lord Jesus Christ. Through him we have obtained access to this grace in which we stand, and we rejoice in our hope of sharing the glory of God. More than that, we rejoice in our sufferings, knowing that suffering produces endurance, and endurance produces character, and character produces hope, and

hope does not disappoint us, because God's love has been poured into our hearts through the Holy Spirit who has been given to us. (Romans 5:1–5)

But the fruit of the Spirit is love, joy, peace, patience, kindness, goodness, faithfulness, gentleness, self-control; against such there is no law. (Galatians 5:22–23)

But as for you, man of God, shun all this; aim at righteousness, godliness, faith, love, steadfastness, gentleness. Fight the good fight of the faith; take hold of the eternal life to which you were called when you made the good confession in the presence of many witnesses. (1 Timothy 6:11–12)

When we commit ourselves to cooperate with grace and to live in the light of these virtues, we move from the babyhood of the spiritual life, with its constant swing from egocentric to other-centered love; through the throes of spiritual adolescence, with its tendency to bargain with God ("I'll be good, if you do this favor for me"), to the adulthood of spirituality where we apply Gospel directives to daily life. Doing what Jesus would do becomes second nature to us.

The path to which the virtues described in this book point is that of mature faith and ongoing conversion of heart despite occasional temptations to doubt, uncertainty, and lack of charity. Part One explores the virtues of the inner life like courage and gratitude, all of which implant in our heart continuous lasting dispositions, which affect our character. For example, when we cultivate a grateful heart, we become people who exude appreciation despite the hardships we encounter. Part Two takes up such virtues of the relational life as forgiveness and hospitality. These virtues strengthen the bonds between us, draw us into deeper intimacy with the Lord and with one another, and enkindle mutually supportive decisions and deeds of love and service. Part Three integrates virtuous living with the situations in which we find ourselves on a day-to-day basis. We need to grow in patience and perseverance. Without these virtues we may become impatient when we have to handle annoying situations like facing long lines in the supermarket or feeling incapable of carrying on with a task when too many obstacles present themselves. Part Four makes us attentive to the fact that we share the same earth and that we ought not to take advantage of anyone. That is why, for example, we need to be more generous, just, loyal, and serene. Revealing the challenges we must face due to the proliferation of vices in our personal and social lives is the purpose of the Appendix.

This book as a whole teaches us that to live virtuously is to trust totally in the providence of God. As a result, we begin to live in serenity of soul, undisturbed by vices that tempt us to make our ego projects more important than God's guidance. Lifted from our shoulders like a heavy weight are excessive worry, destructive gossip, and undue meddling. We are less likely to become so preoccupied with this or that plan or project that we forget how dependent we are on God. Virtuous living teaches us the primacy of the love relationship that exists between us and our Creator. God knows that we are liable to act like sick souls who need to be healed in the hospice of forgiveness and compassion. We journey from the state of unlikeness to Christ, where we are entrenched in pride, to the state of likeness to Christ. We do not rest in the complacency of having arrived but in the faith and hope that we are always arriving. We try our best to walk in the truth of who we are, following the threefold path recommended in *The Way of Perfection* by St. Teresa of Avila of humility, detachment, and fraternal charity. We embrace the Cross and await the joy of Easter Morning. We adopt the conviction characteristic of adult discipleship that by clinging to Jesus and radiating Gospel revelations, our lives are less likely to deviate from the direction intended for us by God.

The *penthos* (conversion) of a contrite heart enables the regenerative experience of ongoing conversion. Spirit, heart, mind, and will feel renewed, revived, and ready to radiate the values Christ teaches. By virtue of this regenerated outlook, we see in our life situations pointers to the meaning God has in mind for our life as a whole. We appreciate the awesome truth that what happens from the moment of conception to the moment of transition to eternity is part of the unfolding of our unique-communal call (vocation) to oneness in the Lord.

Conversion is a lifelong story. It does not preclude the temptations associated with spiritual babyhood or the brakes put on our tendency to disobey God during spiritual adolescence: "We will be led in the night of faith into a profound confrontation with ourselves—with the best and the worst in us. We cannot hide from God nor turn away from our destiny."[1] What matters is not that we occasionally miss the mark but that we are sorry to have done so; we are willing to start again on the road to spiritual maturity. Only over the life span from birth to death will the implications of our call become clear. What we seek is not instant conversion, which fades with the dawn, but a well-tested faith that, thanks to the grace of God, refuses to turn back.

The legacy that Jesus leaves us bears emulating in this and every age. Generosity, zeal, and charity lead necessarily to feeding the hungry, banishing the evil one, and practicing humility. Jesus' final days witness to the cost of discipleship, which demands radical obedience, total abandonment to God, and love that knows no bounds. Sacrifice for the sake of salvation softens the sting of suffering and gives way to joy.

I wrote this book because what surrounds us like the air we breathe is more often than not vice and the vicious behavior it breeds. Were an electronic calculator posted on a billboard for the purpose of recording how many times evil appears to triumph over good the results would be devastating. People who ought to know better—evangelists, economists, politicians—fall headlong into lust, avarice, and dismaying double-talk. Lying becomes not an occasional slip of the tongue but a way of life.

This text does not purport to halt such a tidal wave of sin and selfishness. Its aim is to reveal the lasting value of living a good life. It gathers together, like the ingredients for an award-winning recipe,

---

1 Susan Muto and Adrian van Kaam, *Divine Guidance: Seeking to Find and Follow the Will of God* (Pittsburgh, PA: Epiphany Books, 2000), 71 –72.

the virtuous decisions and actions that promote both the individual and the common good inwardly, relationally, in our here-and-now situation, and on a global scale.

Wisdom, according to Solomon, is the key to virtuous living (cf. Wisdom 10), which guides us along the right paths of goodness and sincerity of heart. A disciplined spirit flees from deceit and leaves foolish thoughts behind (cf. Wisdom 1:5). The list of virtues mentioned in the Bible in the Wisdom of Solomon counsels us to practice kindliness, justice, genuine enjoyment, generosity to the poor, righteousness, peace, and fear of the Lord. These are only a few of the reasons why those who walk in God's light "will receive great good, because God tested them and found them worthy of himself" (Wisdom 3:5). Virtuous souls, says Solomon, "run like sparks through the stubble." They govern nations and their style of ruling becomes legendary. They are the women and men, the people of God, "who trust in him," who "understand truth," who "abide with him in love" (Wisdom 3:7–9).

Aided by the formative reading of Holy Scripture, by meditation, prayer, and contemplation, my intention is to present in the following pages a blueprint for virtuous living. I will try with God's help to offer a formula of sorts for replacing pride with humility, envy with respect, anger with patience, lust with chastity, sloth with perseverance, avarice with generosity, and gluttony with poverty of spirit—all culminating in a life of gratitude and joy, of hope and peace. My reason for writing can be found in the words of Solomon: "[G]race and mercy are upon his elect, and [God] watches over his holy ones" (Wisdom 3:9).

INTRODUCTION

PART ONE
VIRTUES OF THE INNER LIFE

Adoration
Detachment
Fidelity
Humility
Repentance
Courage
Gratitude

To practice these virtues is to change our heart so that with God's help we can change our lives, starting with the move from arrogance to adoration, the first building block of a well formed, reformed, and transformed character.

CHAPTER 1
ADORATION

O come, let us worship and bow down,
let us kneel before the Lord, our Maker! (Psalm 95:6)

The virtue of adoration is in many ways the wellspring from whence flows, like a trickling stream into a mighty river, the entire repertoire of all that constitutes the good life. If we love God with our whole spirit, body, mind, and will, then, as the Great Commandment says, we will love our neighbors as we love ourselves.

Adoration is like a magnet that attracts to itself a constellation of companion virtues ranging from the "ah!" of sheer grace to the wordless wonder felt when we view the sun-washed crevices of the Grand Canyon. To the degree that we adore God, we can delight in His law and meditate on it day and night (cf. Psalm 1:2). Once adoration moves from our lips, through our mind, to our heart; the other virtues of the inner life meld together to form our character. We become more obedient to what the Lord asks of us out of love, not fear. We banish from our attention the deceptive thoughts that collect around such vices as arrogance, anger, and avarice. They lose their power to deceive us once we accept the truth that the key to lasting happiness is adoration of God to whom we bow in humility. We relinquish the illusion of our having total control over anything. We acknowledge that without God we can do nothing.

By contrast, non-adorers, as Solomon tells us, invest their interest in the pursuit of wickedness; they become the victims of roving desires bent on perverting innocent minds (cf. Wisdom 4:12). Alas, they reap what they sow. In the end, the Lord laughs them to scorn; they become "dishonored corpses," shaken from their faulty foundations and left "utterly dry and barren" (Wisdom 4:18–19). In short, they turn this virtue into the vice of self-adoration.

The task we all face is to name our idols and then to smash them to pieces for God's sake. This first step toward conversion puts us on the road to virtuous character formation. Adoration disinclines us ever to take God for granted. Forgetful though we may be of our true destiny, we try to follow the Apostle Paul's admonition that "at the name of Jesus every knee should bow, in heaven and on earth and under the earth, and every tongue confess that Jesus Christ is Lord, to the glory of God the Father" (Philippians 2:10–11).

This text calls to mind an encounter I had in the Holy Land with a devout Muslim. In the course of our conversation he made this startling observation: "If I walked into any one of your Christian Churches and saw a candle burning near the tabernacle to announce the real presence of God among us, I would lie prostrate on the floor in abject adoration." How casually, by contrast, we enter the sanctuary, often not having enough reverence to keep silent and worship the Lord.

Adoration enables us to stand in awe before the One whom we cannot see or touch but in whom we believe. Its companion virtue is moral and spiritual acquiescence. We know we are not in charge of anything. God is our all in all. Much to our amazement, the Hidden Mystery whom we adore seeks intimacy with us. In response to this holy initiative, we have to become single-hearted lovers, humbly accepting the grace that alone can release us from the bondage of self-love.

In the Book of Chronicles, we find an excellent example of virtuous character building in King Asa (cf. 2 Chronicles 14:1–14). During the ten years of his leadership, Israel was at peace. He decided from the beginning of his reign that he would do exactly what the Lord asked of His people in the First Commandment. He would not allow any false god to take the place of God. He and his subjects would live in adoration and obedience.

At the end of ten years, coinciding with the end of Asa's reign, all was well, that is, until he made one fatal mistake. He did not realize that the true test of his character would entail not the smashing of heathen idols, important as this act was, but the smashing of the idols in his own heart. As the Book of Chronicles relates, Asa did not rely on God to help him win the battle, but began relying on himself. The minute he did so, the break he had dreaded occurred between him and God. For King Asa raised up the largest idol of all: his own pride.

Notice well. At the start Asa did what was good and pleasing to God. He removed the heathen altars and the idols on high places. He broke to pieces and cut down the sacred poles that paid homage to gods and goddesses other than the God of Abraham, Isaac, and Jacob, the God whom the people had been commanded alone to adore. Asa commanded Israel to observe to the letter the law God had decreed.

There is a lesson for us in Asa's story. As we try to craft our character in the form of the person God wants us to be, it is good to check out whether or not we have the courage to see into our prideful hearts and remove this idol of idols. What are the pagan altars we have unwittingly built up within our own lives? Are they altars to material goods? To having everything go our way? To tempting God to conform to our bargains and demands?

Whatever the idol may be, are we willing to break it into bits, as Asa initially did? Consider your answer carefully. When you smash an idol you have built, it will hurt your pride. When you cast aside your self-woven security blankets, you may feel painfully vulnerable. When your life shatters into pieces, you may be whiplashed by anger, self-pity, and a sense of defeat. But learn to trust the process of divine transformation. God can make something beautiful out of even broken bits if we agree to wait upon the mystery. Soon we may see in these obstacles a formation opportunity.

The main force opposing this posture of humble presence is false pride, not a superficial kind of boasting or showing off, but a much deeper problem. Pride is the basic inclination to believe that "I" or "we" can do it alone. People with this problem often harbor beneath the surface of such brash behavior hidden fears and feelings of insecurity. They need to control things so much so that pride, understood as total self-sufficiency, gets the best of them.

Such pride is at the root of our fallen condition. It is the original sin described in Genesis. It was not enough for Adam and Eve to be like God; they would *be* "gods." The result of their disobedience in eating the forbidden fruit was not joy but despair, not peace but disruption. The myth that "I," on my own power, can make "myself" whole is a sure formula for failure. Placing false gods before God banishes the possibility of intimacy with the divine, and therewith, of lasting happiness.

To move from false pride to true praise means to love God as our first priority and to admire, never abuse, the good people and things God has made—the friends and family around us, the challenges that face us, the gifts the Adored grants us. We must first praise God if we are to survive as a people, humanly speaking. This praise is only possible if we do not hold on to lesser goods too tightly. To be willing to let go is not easy. We must try to swallow our pride and praise God if we want to enjoy the happiness of an undivided, humble heart.

A primary condition for living in adoration is that we stop trying to play God. There is no shortcut to obeying the love-will of the divine (God's will) in our everyday life. There is no shout from heaven, only an appeal to read as prayerfully as we can the signals God sends to light our way on this first step to virtuous living.

LET US PRAY

Lord, in Your mercy, awaken in my overly complacent heart the virtue of adoration. Wipe away the stains of arrogance that obscure the radiance of awe. In the presence of Your mystery, draw me to my knees and keep me there until I realize in whose presence I am. Let me search my heart to find whether or not it belongs to You alone. Transform me, as You did the Samaritan woman, into a worshipper in spirit and in truth (John 4:24), who believes what I have heard and who bows in fear and trembling before the Adored One, the Savior of the World.

CHAPTER 2

DETACHMENT

Be still, and know that I am God. (Psalm 46:10)

The beauty of the virtuous life is that one building block interlocks with the other. Adoration is inconceivable without the willingness to let go of our own agendas. Detachment means literally to "de-tack" from the parameters of our existence whatever prevents us from giving God the first priority. A great master of this virtue, St. John of the Cross, reminds us that it matters not if we are entrapped in excessive attachments by a thin thread or a heavy chain. As long as these shackles bind us to things rather than to the God who made them, we cannot enjoy the freedom of spirit God intends for us.[1]

In *The Ascent of Mount Carmel* the Saint details what he means. How regrettable that a soul laden like a rich vessel with the wealth of good deeds, spiritual exercises, and virtues never leaves port because one lacks the courage to break the rope of a little satisfaction, attachment, or affection. God gives us the power to sever stronger cords while we cling to some childish act or object that God asks us to relinquish for the sake of love. Not only do we fail to advance, we turn back for something that amounts to no more than a thread or a hair. As the Saint says, "everyone knows that not to go forward on this road is to turn back, and not to gain ground is to lose."

---

1 *The Ascent of Mount Carmel* in *The Collected Works of St. John of the Cross*, trans. Kieran Kavanaugh and Otilio Rodriguez (Washington, DC: ICS Publications, 1991), Book One, Chapter 11:4, 143.

The goal of union demands that we mortify our appetites rather than indulge them. How can a log of wood be transformed into fire if a single degree of heat is lacking to its preparation? No wonder this master contends that the soul will not be transformed in God even if it has only one imperfection. This is so because a person has only one will, and if it is encumbered or occupied by anything, it will not possess the freedom, solitude, and purity of heart requisite for divine transformation.

St. John concludes paradoxically that only by entering into *nothingness* can we enter into *nothing-butness*—for nothing but God will satisfy our restless longings.[2] Practiced with order and discretion, mortifications can facilitate our living in faithfulness to our unique call. What is easiest and what is most difficult depends, of course, on who we are. It may be easiest for a research scientist not to spend tedious hours in his laboratory looking for formulas that will benefit human health when he would rather be on the golf course. Hence, what is difficult and to be done for Christ by the scientist is to maintain his place in the lab, utilizing to the full his God-given talents. For another person, the most difficult chore may be to overcome her shyness and meet colleagues on the golf course, to temper her workaholic tendency and relax for a change.

Detachment, in other words, has to be "in sync" with who we are. To engage in what Adrian van Kaam calls "syntonic mortification," we must exercise the appraisal powers of our transcendent mind and will.[3] Supporting these faculties and guaranteeing prudence is the basic counsel of St. John's dictum, "Endeavor to be inclined always" to imitate Christ and to be ready to do what is most in keeping with our call to discipleship[4].

A heart detached from anything less than God frees us to let God use our senses and spirit, our gifts and talents for the good of others. Detachment from what entraps us increases our energy and fosters that loving abandonment to the mystery that transforms our

---

2 Cf. Ibid., Book One, Chapter 13:11.
3 See Adrian van Kaam, *The Transcendent Self* (Pittsburgh, PA: Epiphany Association, 1991).
4 *The Ascent of Mount Carmel*, Book One, Chapter 13:6, 149.

character. It saves us from the obstacle of Easing God Out *(EGO)* of our lives by not practicing conformity to Christ and growing in humility and detachment simultaneously. This latter virtue leaves us less dispersed and more integrated. Only in this act of self-emptying can we experience the grace of equanimity.

Detachment calms the whirlwind of covetous desires that plague us in a consumer society; it reminds us of our dependence on the divine in prosperity and adversity. What causes us to toss to and fro like a hingeless screen door is any inordinate attachment to persons, events, and things that we think of as ends in themselves, rather than as pointers to the "More Than."

Complementary virtues that foster detachment and enable us to put God's will before all else denote further steps to inner liberation. The first is to "re-member" all that is as dependent on God. The second is to "compare" the finite, limited nature of what we see to the "how much more" of the Infinite in whom we believe. For example, the Pacific Ocean compared to the sea of God's love is like a drop of water left in the bottom of a glass. It can never quench our thirst for the transcendent. The third is to "renounce" whatever enthralls us to the point of forgetfulness of the Sacred. We need to detach ourselves from these lesser goods for the sake of attaching ourselves to what is more than they can ever be. When we cast off our self-woven security blankets, we are bound to feel vulnerable, but out of these broken bits emerges a beauty unlike any other. Through the virtue of detachment, God begins to wean the soul away from consolations granted in the babyhood of the spiritual life towards a mature relationship with the God who consoles.

LET US PRAY

Lord, let me not be so laden with a wealth of good deeds and spiritual disciplines that I forget to rest in You. Give me the motivation I need to sever the chains that bind me to whatever diverts my attention from what You ask of me. Teach me to detach myself from all that eases You out of my life. Let the space created in my heart be the place where You come to dwell. Loosen my bonds and set me free to go wherever Your Spirit leads me.

CHAPTER 3
FIDELITY

If you will not believe, surely you shall not be established. (Isaiah 7:9)

According to St. John of the Cross, faith—not works, not ecstatic experiences, only faith—can be the eagle that carries us to union with God[1]. Not only must we let go of power, pleasure, and possession for God's sake, we must also, in the process of detachment, lean on naked faith alone. Faith, like a secret ladder, is often hidden from the senses (we believe, though we do not see) and from the spirit (we choose life over death, though once in a while we may not know why or for what). Often God asks us to make a leap of faith and to let Him lead us to a vantage point where we may be able to behold, albeit through a glass darkly, the deepest reason to hope and trust in times of tribulation. The ladder we climb may shake a bit, but faith makes us feel secure. This theological virtue gives us the confidence to persevere in our upward ascent to God.

Why does St. John compare faith to "midnight" rather than to "twilight" or "dawn"? Faith, he says, is an "obscure habit" that brings one to a belief in divinely revealed truths, which transcend every natural light and infinitely exceed all human understanding. The light of faith in its abundance, like the light of the sun, both dazzles and darkens, suppresses and overwhelms the light of the human intellect.

1 *The Ascent of Mount Carmel*, Book Two, Chapter 2:1, 155–156.

What it offers as its object is simply too much for the intellect with its logical powers to comprehend. The intellect can master perceived knowledge—as a person can solve an equation—but only through faith does it have the potential to rise to supernatural insight in accordance with the revelations of Holy Scripture.

We can reappreciate the need for fidelity by calling to mind that there is perhaps no more hurtful vice known to humanity than infidelity. To give one's word to another and not to keep it results in a demeaning act of betrayal, far beneath the dignity of a person created in the image and likeness of God.

Fidelity, by contrast, is as humanizing as infidelity is dehumanizing. Along with hope and charity, it binds us to the Trinity and makes the dream of discipleship a reality, on the condition, of course, that we drop our previously scripted plans and consent to follow the delicate unfolding of divine providence.

Faith lets us see beyond the bounds of human reason to the supernatural revelations of God. It is the wing of truth that welcomes us into the hidden chambers of our filial adoption in the family of the Trinity (cf. Galatians 4:5). To say "I believe" is to go beyond what we can grasp of the revelation by virtue of our intellect or imagination. Faith draws us from the comprehensible to what is incomprehensible by the efforts of reason alone. The most we may feel and taste of God in this life is infinitely distant from the embrace of transforming love in which we live and move and have our being (cf. Acts 17:28).

The way of faith is at once simple and complex. Simple because it only requires that we say, "Yes, Father, your will, not mine, be done"; complex because the demon of doubt tempts us not to accept our limits and losses without falling into the quicksand of self-pity and chronic disappointment.

Faith diminishes our need to push against the pace of grace and to risk losing our peace. Just as hope empties our memory of past hurts, just as charity deprives us of outlandish attachments to self, not God, so faith encourages us to see in every ending a new beginning, all the while knowing that God is at our side (cf. Psalm 124:1).

To climb the mount of conformity to Christ, we must travel lightly. To seek and gain God, we must soar free. We must run, not walk, through the narrow gate onto the straight path. To remain sensitive to the needs of others, we must cooperate with the grace of selflessness; to carry this responsive orientation over to the spiritual realm, we must grow strong in purity of heart and poverty of spirit. These intentions may lead us to walk on the less-traveled road, but we do not do so alone. God's own Son, the second Person of the Blessed Trinity, Emmanuel, is with us smoothing the rough edges and fording the wildest streams.

LET US PRAY

Lord, let the faith I profess be the underlying theme of my journey from birth to death. I ask You in childlike trust for the grace to say with the Apostle Paul, "I have fought the good fight, I have finished the race, I have kept the faith" (2 Timothy 4:7). Let no egocentric impediment or deceptive ploy stand in the way of my quest for oneness with You. Illumine the shadows in my mind with lights of insight and understanding that could never be mine without the gift of faith. Let me follow You with the confidence that quells every doubt, with the loyalty that silences every lying tongue.

CHAPTER 4
HUMILITY

For the fear of the Lord is wisdom and instruction, and
he delights in fidelity and meekness. (Sirach 1:27)

The fourth virtue of the inner life is humility. Without it we would not be able to adore God, to let go of our self as the center of the universe, and to accept in faith what God reveals to us. Nor would we ever submit to persecution and misunderstanding without complaint, as Jesus did.

St. Teresa of Avila describes this virtue as a queen highly pleasing to His Majesty. In her masterpiece *The Interior Castle*[1], she says that humility means to walk in the truth of who we are.

In *The Way of Perfection*[2], she concludes that this virtue embraces all the others because it counters the one vice that most separates us from God, pride or vainglory. In one of her most memorable comparisons, she depicts humility as the queen in a game of chess:

> The queen is the piece that can carry on the best battle in this game, and all the other pieces help. There's no queen like humility for making the King surrender. Humility drew the King from heaven to the womb of

---

1 *The Interior Castle* in *the Collected Works of St. Teresa of Avila*, trans. Kieran Kavanaugh and Otilio Rodriguez (Washington, DC: ICS Publications, 1980), The Sixth Dwelling Places, Chapter 10:7, 420–421.

2 Ibid., *The Way of Perfection*, Chapter 4:4, 54.

the Virgin, and with it, by one hair we will draw Him to our souls. And realize that the one who has more humility will be the one who possesses Him more; and the one who has less will possess Him less. For I cannot understand how there could be humility without love or love without humility; nor are these two virtues possible without detachment from all creatures. (Chapter 16:2, 94)

In other words, Teresa treats this triad of virtues—humility, detachment, and charity—as the royal road to a life of union with God. Humility undergirds our readiness to be content with whatever God allows, not going higher without His prevenient grace and not falling lower out of fear of the unknown. Humility is false when it leads us to deny our gifts, and true when we use them for the honor and glory of God, all the while admitting that we are but useless servants, striving to combine wisdom with down-to-earth works.

Humility is less a matter of focusing on our misery and more a way of becoming aware of the truth that without God we are and can do nothing (cf. John 15:5). To grow in the humble integration of sanctity and service, we must try to take in stride whatever His holy providence asks of us, however lowly it may seem. St. Teresa enjoyed peeling the potatoes for the sisters' supper as much as setting off to establish a new Carmelite convent. Washing pots and pans in the monastery kitchen gave Brother Lawrence of the Resurrection as much joy as counseling his brothers in the practice of the presence of God. There was one smooth flow from the Teresa of Calcutta who bathed dying Hindus to the future saint who accepted the Nobel Prize for peace. Holy women like these two Teresas teach us that humble service never fails to draw us closer to God. As companions of Christ, they bore unjust accusations with dignity and non-defensiveness. They accepted to be misunderstood without retaliatory cynicism because their first love was for the Cross.

It is impossible to take our lead from Jesus and not be alert to the slightest sign of self-exaltation. His Spirit helps us to become proficient in detecting the lure of a "me-centered" existence and to choose instead the "narrow way" (Matthew 7:14). Rather than regarding equality with God as an honor to be grasped, the Lord "humbled himself and became obedient unto death . . . on a cross" (Philippians 2:8). The study of ecclesial history, as well as sheer observation of our present circumstances, convinces us that the promise to be a friend of Jesus is to incur suffering of some sort. The cross may be experienced when we come up against personal limitations, when we have to admit our inability to fulfill cherished plans, when we are the brunt of misunderstanding. It stings us in the uneventful routines of daily living, in our powerlessness to help certain people, and in our failure to change ourselves when we know it is time to do so. As the founder of Methodism, John Wesley, once said in a sermon on the theme of salvation, "None sin because they do not have grace, but because they do not use the grace they have."[3] Some form of suffering is bound to be our accepted lot if we walk the way Christ has chosen for us. Acceptance of this suffering is what makes us sharers in Christ's redeeming love.

Every true follower of the Suffering Servant has to expect affliction in this life and welcome it as an opportunity to become spiritually mature. This is inherent in Christ's invitation to take up our cross and follow Him. With the help of the Holy Spirit, our first response may be prayerful abandonment to God's will, combined with the firm belief that Christ will give us the strength we need to see this crisis through with humility and constancy.

Without the example of Jesus' own self-emptying, we would be hard-pressed to deny ourselves, take up our cross, and follow Him (cf. Matthew 16:24). To live in humility is to enjoy a life directed inwardly to God and outwardly to others. Empty of possessiveness, egoism, and pride through God's progressive action of purification, we find a new sense of freedom. The paradox of renunciation is that it leads us to liberation. Rather than clinging to what we possess as if it

---

3 See his collection of forms of prayer for every day of the week (1733) in *John and Charles Wesley, Selected Writings and Hymns*, eds. Frank Whaling and Albert Outler (New York: Paulist Press, 1981), 77–84.

were ours, we celebrate life as God's gift. As the saints say, we possess everything because we know we possess nothing. All belongs to God and all must be returned to God. We are to keep nothing for ourselves; however while on earth, it is our duty to use God's gifts wisely and with gratitude. We bow before God in awe, humbly acknowledging the divine Giver, who asks us to rid ourselves of "all filthiness and rank growth of wickedness and receive with meekness the implanted word, which is able to save [our] souls" (James 1:21).

LET US PRAY

Lord, open the eyes of my heart so that I may see in the limits of my being countless blessings. Let the seeds of holiness planted in hiddenness be harvested in humility. Make me a meek or God-molded person. Give me the courage to walk in the truth of who I am and to be the person You made me. Warn me when vainglory strikes my heart. Remind me that those who exalt themselves will be humbled (Luke 14:11). Teach me what Mary our Mother experienced—that You cast down the mighty from their thrones and lift up the lowly (Luke 1:52).

CHAPTER 5

REPENTANCE

The Lord is not slow about his promise as some count slowness,
but is forbearing toward you, not wishing that any should perish,
but that all should reach repentance. (2 Peter 3:9)

With vice being only a breath away, it is no wonder that
repentance is essential for virtuous living. The Apostle Paul's
words in this regard offer us both a tale of encouragement and of
caution: "I do not understand my own actions. For I do not do what
I want, but I do the very thing I hate. . . . For I do not do the good
I want, but the evil I do not want is what I do" (Romans 7:15, 19).

The virtue of repentance has the double effect of evoking a deep
sense of regret for all the ways in which we have spurned God's
offer of unconditional love and of revealing the infinite reaches of
divine mercy. It connotes a commingling of sorrow for sin and joy
in forgiveness. Lacking repentance, our progress in the spiritual life
might grind to a halt. Either we would turn a blind eye to our faults or
go to the opposite extreme of inflicting upon ourselves harsh penances
in the conviction that they will save us. Unfortunately, self-sought
perfectionism only leads to further despair.

The anonymous author of the fourteenth century English classic
The Cloud of Unknowing wisely advises us not to concentrate too
much on minute details concerning what we have done or failed to
do, but to focus on our being a "lump of sin" in need of forgiveness.
The author, a renowned spiritual director, includes in his counsels the

necessity of a prayerful examination of our conscience. We must seek reconciliation with God by honestly confessing a particular moral failing we desire to overcome or by focusing on a virtue we want to exercise with the help of grace.

Repentance neither mitigates our need to make a fresh start nor leaves us feeling too ashamed of our behavior to ask for God's help. It teaches us to avoid the swing from being easy going about sin to falling into self-punishing scrupulosity. The latter feeling can so escalate false guilt that it prompts us to think we must first be perfect since only then can God love us.

Repentance is the balancing agent that enables us to avoid these extremes. We find consolation in God's compassion as well as the courage to take responsibility for our sinfulness. Repentant hearts shift from the remorse of contrition to the restoration of confidence in the saving love of God, which renews in us "a willing spirit" (Psalm 51:12).

The Eastern Church fathers taught that *penthos* or compunction was the one virtue that could save us from sin and separation from God. *Penthos* is the starting point of *metanoia* or conversion of heart. David, the Shepherd-King, could follow the call of God only when he admitted, "I have sinned" (2 Samuel 12:13). Peter could avoid the despair that claimed Judas' life only when he acknowledged his betrayal of the Lord and, full of repentance, "went out and wept bitterly" (Luke 22:62).

In his autobiography, *The Confessions*, St. Augustine shows that contrition leads to conversion. He raises compunction from a feeling of sorrow for sin to an invitation to seek union with Christ whose Cross we share. The sins that once enthralled him became signs used by God to lead him to repent and seek redemption. Illumined by this virtue, the providential design of his life at last began to make sense. Here was a sinner destined by God to become a great saint.

When we repent, it is as if the refreshing rain of divine mercy falls upon the arid desert of our misery. When we move toward God with contrition of heart, God rushes to meet us as the father met, with outstretched arms of love, His prodigal son (cf. Luke 15:11–32).

Every time we tend to lose our way, we should exercise *penthos* and ponder God's promise with renewed peace: "Truly, truly, I say to you, you will weep and lament, but the world will rejoice; you will be sorrowful, but your sorrow will turn into joy" (John 16:20).

LET US PRAY

Lord, may I find a way neither to presume too much upon Your mercy nor to feel unworthy of forgiveness. Catch me when I fall into the traps of self-centered defensiveness or paralyzing doubt about your ever-present mercy. Grant me the grace of receptivity to the slightest stirrings of repentance. Block any thought that tempts me to believe that I am not worthy of redemption and restore in me the joy of Your salvation.

CHAPTER 6
COURAGE

Be watchful, stand firm in your faith, be courageous,
be strong. (1 Corinthians 16:13)

Courage like the French word "le coeur" is a core virtue at the heart of Christian character formation. It is the unshakeable stance that prevents us from being persuaded to betray our principles. Courage deters us from swaying to the clamorous tune of the crowd or from forfeiting our freedom by conforming to the impersonal demands of a faceless collective.

Courage is the fountainhead from whence flows the determination to follow the dictates of the Gospel under all circumstances. The yes of a courageous person means yes, and his or her no means no. Wishy-washy "maybes" give way to bold decisions that make a difference in this world.

Courage bolsters fidelity to one's marital promises when the honeymoon is over. It issues a reality check to those utopian enthusiasms that come and go, and plants our feet on the firm, reliable foundations of virtuous living. It enables us to press on in the face of unfair opposition and unrepentant deception. It enlivens our sense of mission and helps us to hold a steady course amidst the vicissitudes of time.

It takes courage to set our sights on the horizon that lies beyond the obstacles strewn on our path; to exercise to the full our gifts and

31

skills; to function at the peak of our performance when we see others in the workplace compromising the pursuit of excellence. Henry David Thoreau wrote in *Walden* that it is one thing to dream our dreams and another to muster the courage to put solid foundations under them. Only then can we act with what St. Teresa of Avila dubbed "determined determination."

When Dietrich Bonhoeffer stripped naked and walked in advance of his captors to the wall of execution, he became a model of Christian courage worthy of universal emulation. We see in such acts of bravery that courage not only bolsters our sense of purpose, it also protects us from becoming indifferent to the suffering of others. It sensitizes us to the slightest deviation from our original intention to follow the commands of the Lord with gentle yet firm resolve.

The occasional discouragement we feel when we seem to be making little or no progress in our spiritual, social, or professional life may put a damper on this virtue. That is the time to muster the courage that carried us through trying times. It helps to set our sights on the sense of purpose that guided us thus far. Bolstered by a good memory from the past, we can move more courageously toward the future. What held us back was the illusion of control. Courage reminds us that to go forward we must abandon ourselves to the direction set by the providence of God. Rather than trying to forecast what might occur were we in charge, we wait courageously upon the always better plan of God. This renewal of courage is not a once-and-for-all event but a process that unfolds over a lifetime since all too often cowardice licks at our heels. In the drabness of passing days as well as in the delights of unexpected surprises, we strive to emulate the courage of our dying and rising Lord, making His actions the focal point of our decisions.

Singer and artist Tony Bennett made a good point in this regard in an interview published in a February 1992 issue of *Parade Magazine.* Asked if he could live his life over again, would he do anything differently, he replied:

> Whatever I am, I accept it. There are a lot of things I
> don't know or things I ever will, but I try to sketch and

learn as much as I can. I don't regret anything. You see, the great thing about painting is that a lot of paintings don't work, and it dramatizes what happens in life. When you first start painting, and it doesn't work out, you're devastated. But you keep painting. Then you're not bothered by your mistakes. You just say, "The next time will be better." That's what happens in life. That's why I wouldn't change anything. . . . I made mistakes, but those mistakes taught me how to live.

Courage gives new meaning to setbacks and sorrows. It enables us to cope with rough spots on the road ahead, to swerve around potholes, and to ask an expert when we lose our sense of direction. Stamina increases with every honest assessment of our mistakes. Doors may close but windows stay open to courageous hearts willing to grow.

LET US PRAY

Lord, may Your Paschal Mystery be the compass that carries me beyond the death knell of discouragement to the rousing church bells announcing the dawning of a new day. Strengthen me to be the kind of person who seeks Your glory and the good You ordain despite pain and persecution. Open my heart to those horizons of grace by which You show me that yesterday, today, and tomorrow shine with transcendent meaning.

CHAPTER 7
GRATITUDE

I will thank you for ever, because you have done it. (Psalm 52:9)

The virtue of gratitude can best be appreciated when we consider its counterpart: ingratitude. It changes an otherwise pleasant face into a dour frown. Whining and complaining create habits of the heart that erode good humor. Ungrateful outlooks banish upbeat smiles and dim our vision of what can be. Lack of appreciation attunes our inner radar system to what is wrong with everyone. We fail to see that the cause of this disgust resides in our own heart.

By contrast, gratitude provides us with an inner detection system that picks up the first bleep of bad moods and redirects them in a more positive light. We laugh at the mountain of dejection we have made out of the molehill of momentary misunderstanding. We defocus on what causes us to feel stressed and focus instead on the foibles of the human condition that ought to evoke compassion.

Giving thanks is after all a biblical directive. The people of God are to bring Him thanksgiving offerings (cf. 2 Chronicles 29:31); they are to "give thanks to the Lord, for he is good" (Psalm 107:1); with thanksgiving they are to let their requests be made known to God (cf. Philippians 4:6). This virtue remains a wellspring of happiness despite momentary down swings of depression. It outlasts the pleasure principle and the fleeting satisfaction of passing success.

Gratitude transcends the ups and downs of daily life that challenge us but can never defeat us. It enables us to see, amidst inevitable deprivations, such as those associated with the aging process, that in every loss there is a seed of gain. This light-hearted disposition readies us when Plan A does not work to go to Plan B. It detects in every roadblock a way to unblock it. Grateful hearts tend to let go of frustrations, anger, resentment, envy, and joylessness, if possible, in the blink of an eye.

Flowing with the grace of gratitude has a beneficial effect on every level of our being. Our appraisal of people, events, and things changes for the better thanks to the power of appreciation. It bolsters our ability to make the best of bad deals. We accept the fact that life is never a rose garden free of thorns. No sooner do we plant seeds than weeds spring up beside the flowers. The attitude of gratitude deepens in the face of the imperfect reality of the human condition. We train ourselves not to allow a temporary sting to mushroom into a stubborn, depreciative response. We choose instead to make the shift to appreciative thinking the most compelling motivation behind all that we decide and do.

LET US PRAY

Lord, whenever an ungrateful turn of attention blocks the benevolent vision of my grateful heart, grant me the grace to deflect its destructive turn toward depreciation. Keep me away from any atmosphere that chokes off the fresh air of appreciative living. Whenever it seems as if I have hit a wall of pessimism that saps my peace and joy, lead me out of this morass of soul-sickness as soon as possible. Put a smile on my lips and a song in my heart so that I may witness to the truth that God loves a cheerful giver (2 Corinthians 9:7).

PART TWO
VIRTUES OF THE RELATIONAL LIFE

Compassion
Forgiveness
Hospitality
Respect
Gentility
Integrity
Joy

To put these virtues into practice is to improve our relationships with God, self, and others. Harshness gives way to gentility, dishonesty to integrity, and life between us becomes better and better each day.er.

CHAPTER 8

COMPASSION

The compassion of man is for his neighbor, but the
compassion of the Lord is for all living beings. (Sirach 18:13)

Suffering with our own and others' vulnerability is a condition for the possibility of showing compassion. Empathic understanding, not condescending judgment, is our first recourse. Ours becomes a style of care that strives, insofar as possible, never to harm or humiliate anyone, be they family members or casual acquaintances, friends or strangers, benefactors or beggars. In a world plagued by injustice, genocide, and every form of shameful abuse, we acknowledge in compassion that we are our brothers' and sisters' keepers (cf. Genesis 4:9).

Listen to the nightly broadcasters, tune in to radio talk shows, read any daily newspaper, and it's easy to conclude that there is no good news anywhere in the world, only famine, torture, abuse, and death. Is it any wonder that in such a fallen state, compassion must be one of the central virtues of the relational life? A plane crashes. A drive-by shooting occurs. An earthquake wipes out whole villages. Why were some spared and not others? How can fate be so fickle? There is no adequate explanation for the suffering of the innocent. Minds may wobble under the weight of such pain while hearts exude greater compassion, show mercy to those in need, and help carry their burden.

A world without compassion descends into a disgraceful arena of merciless indifference. A world with compassion allows us to empathize with the poor in body and spirit and to do what we can to relieve their plight. In them we see the suffering Christ whose compassion transcends the barricades built by racial and religious prejudice. In the best of times and the worst of times, we pray for the grace to be Christ's healing hands, His soothing voice. Were we in the medical profession, it would be our privilege to give wounded people a new lease on life. Were we members of a mission team in a country plagued by a tyrannical regime, we would do whatever we could to show the people the face of social justice, peace, and mercy. All of us must rise above our instantaneous likes and dislikes, petty debates, and differences of opinion to attend to our common need for care.

The virtue of compassion cannot be stored in a safe compartment to be taken out only if and when a specific need arises. It has to permeate our whole being and become an indelible part of our Christian character. Charitable efforts, however noble, are not enough. Making an impersonal contribution is not the same as becoming directly involved. A child may need a few minutes of our time, even though he or she asks for money to go to the mall. Every relationship improves when we show compassion. St. Peter summarizes this spark of compassion in these memorable words: "Finally, all of you, have unity of spirit, sympathy, love of the brethren, a tender heart and a humble mind. Do not return evil for evil or reviling for reviling; but on the contrary bless, for this you have been called" (1 Peter 3:8–9).

By contrast, judgmentalism, rivalry, and condescension keep us at a distance from one another. They act like sound barriers that cripple our ability to hear another's silent or verbal cry for help. The three virtues that complement compassion are confirmation, cooperation, and communion. Banished is the secret pleasure we used to feel when others failed. Lessened is our interest in the game of envious comparison. Overridden is the isolationist tendency that bred indifference. Our goal is not to make others into the image of whom we think they ought to be but to become for them mirrors of our merciful Lord.

The fourteenth century English mystic Julian of Norwich says in her *Showings* that mercy belongs to the "motherhood of God." It protects, endures, vivifies, heals; it raises up, rewards, and endlessly exceeds what human needs deserve. Compassion displays the vast plenty and generosity of God, in her words, "his wonderful courtesy." It is this quality that dispels our fear and makes us feel like a beloved child held in the arms of God.

LET US PRAY

Lord, may Your tender compassion for me be mirrored in the mercy I offer the wounded who come my way—those abandoned in body and in soul. You showed such compassion for the sick that everyone who approached You in need went away healed. Allow me despite my limits to light up some corner of the universe with compassion. Thank You for the consoling revelation that mercy triumphs over judgment (James 2:13) and that You will never withhold this soothing balm from Your broken, wounded people.

CHAPTER 9
FORGIVENESS

He [the father] has delivered us from the dominion of darkness
and transferred us to the kingdom of his beloved Son, in whom
we have redemption, the forgiveness of sins. (Colossians 1:13–14)

Imagine trying to melt a rock as if it were an ice cube. We can
compare the rock to an unforgiving heart—cold as ice and not
capable of being thawed. Unless this heart of stone becomes a heart
of flesh (cf. Ezekiel 36:26), in short, a forgiving heart, we may never
escape the hardness of unforgiveness and advance in the virtue Jesus
said we ought to exercise towards others not seven times but seventy
times seven (cf. Matthew 18:21–22).

Consider the plight of Peter. When our Lord's hour had come,
when the Master most needed him, Peter denied that he even knew
His name. He must have sensed almost immediately that he would
verge on despair unless His friend forgave him. Having denied Jesus
three times, he wept bitterly (cf. Mark 14:66–72) rather than berating
himself for being a failure. On that fateful day, when Peter and the
risen Lord shared a meal by the sea, forgiveness was better than food.
Having reconfirmed their love for one another, it was time for Peter
to make a fresh start and accept Jesus' commission to feed His lambs
and tend His sheep (cf. John 21:15–19).

Forgiveness is an expansive virtue essential for good relationships
with ourselves as much as with others. Instead of following the example of Jesus, who forgave His accusers from the Cross (cf. Luke 23:34),

all too often we nearly drown in whirlpools of regret or seething cauldrons of revenge. We miss the lifeline God throws to us. While we were yet sinners, Christ came to redeem us (cf. Romans 5:8). Even before we confess our sins, He bestows upon us the grace of forgiveness.

It is tempting to focus on the maltreatment we have received, but Jesus asks us to follow a different course. He shows us by His own actions that forgiveness is the only virtue strong enough to unclog the sludge of old hurts, crippling resentments, lingering bitterness, and hidden pockets of rage. Forgiveness cleans the wounds that still fester in our system due to an event as foolish as feuding. It frees us to seek reconciliation with God and others since Christ Himself has cancelled our debt.

Even though the scribes bristled at what they labeled blasphemous, Jesus continued to speak with authority as when He forgave the sins of the paralytic and said, "Rise, take up your bed and go home" (Mathew 9:6). Jesus passed this forgiving and healing power on to His Church through the Sacrament of Reconciliation. He applies to each of us personally the "forgiveness" He gained by His sacrifice on the Cross. This treasure of forgiveness is ours for the asking. So central is this virtue that St. Teresa of Avila in *The Way of Perfection* begs her sisters to show fortitude in this regard even if they lack it in other virtues. They must pardon their offenders immediately, with great ease, and remain on good terms with them.

Consider the little skirmishes around the dinner table about bothersome habits, picky neighbors, family decisions, eating customs, styles of dress, or political opinions, to say nothing of out-and-out religious wars. Such battles are fought daily because people have not learned the lesson of forgiveness. Blind to the guidance offered by our forgiving Father in heaven, they persist in wounding one another physically and emotionally. Hearts harden like flint. Life loses its meaning. Many wallow in a misery of their own making.

Is it any wonder that we must pray daily for the gift of forgiveness as well as for the willingness to *accept,* even to *expect,* persecution? Such mistreatment is often a sign that we are doing the work of the Lord. In the light of God's forgiveness, trust begins to replace suspicion. Patience softens anger and irritation. Forgiveness quiets our inclination to quick reprisal. Whatever form it takes, verbal and non-verbal, forgiveness feels like warm oil poured on our own and others' wounds. It is sweet balm softening scars of resentment and giving us a new lease on life.

LET US PRAY

Lord, when Your spirit beckons me to swallow my pride and turn the other cheek, let me not hesitate to comply with Your command: to forgive those who trespass against us. May the ice of unforgiveness never flow in my veins. Thaw my heart and save me from the temptation to begrudge others the forgiveness we both need. Renew my life through the grace of reconciliation and let me take advantage of every opportunity to be a more forgiving person.

CHAPTER 10

HOSPITALITY

Contribute to the needs of the saints, practice hospitality. (Romans 12:13)

The virtue of hospitality expands our horizons. It lifts us above the walls of heartless strife or survival of the fittest. It respects duty and its demands, but it leaves room for leisurely dining with family and friends, for welcoming strangers to the table, for sharing a toast in honor of the relationships we most cherish. Hospitality is healing. It brings us, stressed as we are, to a kind of hospital of the soul where all of us hope to feel better. In its embrace, loneliness lessens and joviality increases. We see ourselves and others in the softer light cast by our divine Host. The banquet table of the Lord becomes our ultimate destiny. For a brief moment the veil between the temporal and the eternal parts and we taste and savor the goodness of the Lord (cf. Psalm 34:8).

Hospitality is a relational virtue that guards against hostility in any form—from a snide remark to slamming the door in someone's face. If hospitable people err, it is always on the side of being friendlier than others have come to expect. A good host or hostess always seems to have time to serve us another cup of tea; he or she waits for a conversation to come to its natural end instead of coercing us to conclude. Harshness creeps in when we plan our lives in isolation and ignore the gentle art of homemaking. What makes us sick is a closed off, "I can-do-it-alone" mentality, followed by wild spurts of fawning attentiveness aimed only at ingratiating us to others for personal gain.

The fruits of hospitality have none of these traits. They include fostering a peaceful, inclusive way of life, offsetting the destructive forces of hostility and indifference, believing that a foe can become a friend. In the hospital of the soul there is no room for the death dealing, life-denying exercise of inhospitality. In the midst of productivity or in our final hour, the care and concern modeled in any hospice ought to be the rule of thumb extended to all.

Hospitality heightens our sensitivity to what others need—from material goods to spiritual exchanges. Without this virtue, we might succumb to one-upmanship, backstabbing, and cynicism. Our goal must be not only to host an occasional dinner party or hug a lonely person once in a blue moon but also to make hospitality an habitual practice. We believe and show by our behavior that everyone ought to be treated warmly whatever state of society they represent.

A military officer told me of a moment when food had run low in the unit because their supply train had been sabotaged. One soldier had saved a candy bar, which he sliced into sixteen pieces so everyone had a taste of chocolate. The dank atmosphere of the trenches took on a warmer hue. That gesture brought hope to a band of formerly despondent soldiers. Each bit of candy was like a tiny iron filing attracted by the magnet of hospitality.

This gift teaches us to share with others both from our abundance and our want. It reminds us of our ultimate indigence and dependence on the Lord of hosts, who dined with prostitutes and sinners, conversed with outcasts like the Samaritan woman, and allowed His hungry disciples to eat wheat on the Sabbath (cf. Luke 6:1–5).

Hospitality allows us to be as generous to others as God has been to us. Receiving a hundredfold in return for even the smallest act of kindness (cf. Luke 8:8) is the surprising gift that awaits us when we listen to the Lord. We minister to others only to find that the tables have turned and that they have become the hospitable ones who ministered to us.

LET US PRAY

Lord, in contrast to the discourtesy I receive at times in this dysfunctional world, let me be kind and courteous to everyone I meet. Free me from the hypocrisy of preaching with glowing words in public while withholding in private the hospitality others crave. Replace selfish hoarding with selfless love so that in my company all may taste a morsel from the heavenly banquet table You have prepared for us. Every time I receive hospitality, let me do what I can to pass this gift on to others. May friends and strangers feel at home when they come through my door. Let them sense in my hospitable presence that they are precious in Your sight, that each is a mirror of the Good Shepherd we serve.

CHAPTER 11

RESPECT

Pay all of them their dues, taxes to whom taxes are due,
revenue to whom revenue is due, respect to whom respect
is due, honor to whom honor is due. (Romans 13:7)

To respect someone is to be willing to look lovingly at them rather than to let first impressions rule. Loving another person is not a sentimental feeling as fickle as the wind but a commitment to respect their dignity and to afford them the reverence they deserve as children of God. This loving give-and-take does not mean that we must always be in agreement; we can agree to disagree agreeably. Our vision of life may differ without diminishing our respect for one another's unique-communal calling (vocation) in the Lord.

Loving God and expressing the overflow of this love in respectful relations with others defend us against the disrespectful tendency to force them to fit into our preconceived mold. Our first thought is to create room for them to grow into the wholesome and joyful persons God intends them to be. It is our task to model our relationships on this invitational, non-coercive appeal to be our best self.

To each person we show the respect that ought to be accorded to "another Christ." Beneath the scarred surface of their existence, we see attributes that hardships may damage but not destroy. Our chaste, respectful love goes beyond mere liking or the fickleness of affinity to address the heart and soul of the person.

Respect awakens us to an enlightened way of seeing that leaves room for us to exchange a variety of views. Differences fade the closer we come to respectful consensus. This virtue rests on the assumption of mutual sincerity. We test the waters to reach the truth and never miss an opportunity to learn from one another. We cooperate without compromise of our faith and formation traditions. Respect does not mean to accommodate ourselves out of existence or for the sake of expediency to forsake our religious freedom.

Disrespect traps us in desensitized thoughts and feelings that slap a label on others before they say a word. We are unable to absorb who they really are because we have already put them in their place. Respect reverses this prejudicial tendency. We do not expect others to replicate our attitudes and actions; rather we open ourselves to the maturing venture of the learning process.

Respect makes us as mindful of our own deficiency as of others' mistakes. Differences are not seen as reasons to drift apart but as occasions to be a part of a continuing conversation. In many ways the worst deprivation we can experience is that of being disrespected. Christ redeemed us from this lack of love by accepting others in whatever state of life they presented themselves to Him—from an outcast like Mary Magdalene to a learned Pharisee like Nicodemus. His response to all who came into His sphere of attention was to accept them where they were and to care for them with full respect. He did not break the bruised reed nor quench the quivering flame. The spirit He manifested must become the litmus test of our own way of relating to one another.

While we may not wish to associate with persons who seem to be bigoted, cruel, or full of conceit, we still try to imprint in our minds the scriptural injunction that the sun rises and sets upon the good and the bad and that it rains upon the just and the unjust (cf. Matthew 5:45). We need to cultivate respect for the innate dignity of all people, hating sin but loving sinners. The root of our respect for others is not their behavior but their humanity and its possible redemption.

Though Jesus forgave the woman caught in adultery and in this confirmed in the most respectful way her essential goodness and dignity as a human person, He told her that she was to go and sin no more (cf. John 8:11). She had to restore her self-respect if she wanted to follow His teaching. We do not know what happened to her after her encounter with the Lord, but we can surmise that she became more available to the grace she needed to resist another fall. Like her, our acceptance of God's confirmation of who we most deeply are is the best antidote to the poison disrespect spreads and to the hateful discrimination it breeds.

LET US PRAY

Lord, help me overcome my automatic reaction of disapproval of those whose ways are not my own. Keep alive in me the hope that he or she can change for the better in a climate of respect. The moment another's behavior repels me, replace the rush of disrespect I feel by the willingness to look again as You did—a look that often pierced their heart and led to compunction and conversion. Soften my propensity to judge others too quickly. Help me to respect our common humanity. Remove the shadows of suspicion that shield me from seeing the truth of everyone's essential goodness and the respect it deserves.

CHAPTER 12

GENTILITY

Rejoice in the Lord always; again I will say, Rejoice. Let all men know your forbearance. The Lord is at hand. (Philippians 4:4–5)

What often evokes a gentle response to the otherwise ungentle forces within us is the recognition of how vulnerable we are. In a culture where rough edges abound, ranging from impatience and discourtesy in the marketplace to loud shouting into cell phones and noise pollution everywhere, is it any wonder that we long for a gentler life style, a milder climate of forbearance, a little rest for our weary souls (cf. Mark 6:31).

The virtue of gentleness has both a relaxing and an energizing effect. Whereas cruelty brings out the worst in us, gentility sustains the best in us. The same happens when we replace anger with forgiveness and irritation with patience. Relationships grow stronger by virtue of beneficent looks, exchanges beyond words, kind gestures conscious of avoiding hurt. Gentleness includes acceptance of our own and others' failings, a mellowing of erratic outbursts of temper, and a readiness to express mutual pardon.

To be avoided at all costs is a posture of pseudo-gentility that replaces genuine concern with a contrived public appearance. This way of relating may be as charming as it is sweetly seductive, but it has as its goal the fulfilling of only selfish purposes. The mask of gentle manners cracks under pressure. Such surface gentility is devoid of other-centered love and service and cannot stand its ground for long. People can spot a phony a mile away.

The deeper our spiritual life becomes, the more likely we are to exude genuine gentility. Tempered step by step, in remembrance of the ways of the Lord, is the tendency to attack others by throwing our weight around, to feel puffed up with our own importance, or to think of kindly people as wimps. Gentleness reverses the harsh thought that we harbor to whip ourselves and others into shape to get ahead in the world. It prevents us from kicking an unruly dog, smashing a dish to show whose kitchen this is, or giving a tongue-lashing to anyone who looks at us with a quizzical eye. Such outbursts may relieve the volcanic anger pent-up inside us, but they do not promote growth in the balance of gentleness and firmness we ought to seek.

Gentleness does not deny or repress anger and aggression. On the contrary, it helps us to bear with volatile feelings we cannot yet overcome. It draws from such affliction the ingredients of honesty and humility that complement a gentle life style. We watch for the first signs of unreasonable indignation that may overtake us. We try not to hurt any person unjustly. Neither do we deny the untender feelings that may overtake us in family and professional life. We prefer to allow them to come to the fore and to be processed in peace before the Lord whose grace we need to grow in gentility. We begin to treat angry interruptions as passing incidents that prick our conscience but do not disrupt the deepest region of our soul where gentleness prevails in respect for the inherent vulnerability of the human condition.

LET US PRAY

Lord, call forth from the core of my being the virtue of gentility. Let the awareness of Your presence instill in my wayward heart a gentle, kind, and courteous care for the whole of creation. When I fail to be gentle, remind me to seek Your healing touch without trying to hide my wounds. In Your tender embrace, let me experience a foretaste of the cordial welcome that awaits me in the eternal homeland toward which I trod ever so gently day after day.

CHAPTER 13
INTEGRITY

The wicked is overthrown through his evildoing, but the righteous finds refuge through his integrity. (Proverbs 14:32)

Like a locomotive rushing out of control, so lack of integrity in our relational life places us in the dangerous position of being neither trusted nor believed. In the letter of Paul to Titus, there are a series of imperatives that reveal the centrality of this virtue and why we must try to maintain it: "Show yourself in all respects a model of good deeds, and in your teaching show integrity, gravity, and sound speech that cannot be censured, so that an opponent may be put to shame, having nothing evil to say of us" (Titus 2:7–8).

Integrity prompts us to show others by our example that we mean what we say and say what we mean. Duplicity—to preach one way and practice another—is a blight we must combat. To perform the good works to which adherence to the Gospel binds us, we must be true to our word. Actions that meet the needs of the moment must arise from a sensible and responsible heart that aligns our decisions with our deeds.

Whether we serve the neighbor next door or needy people around the globe, the same principles recommended by Titus prevail: integrity, gravity, and sound speech. Integrity means to be whole, simple, and straightforward, not scattered in divisive, uncoordinated directions.

This virtue reminds us that the Christian community is to be of one mind and one heart while celebrating the polarity of unity in diversity.

Integrity is not a lightweight virtue; it points to the weighty responsibility each of us must be willing to bear if we are to remain faithful to our calling in Christ. It allows for neither frivolity nor fickleness. Candor is the serious business of promise keepers who honor their commitment to serve God and others without compromise of their or our integrity.

Integrity displays a keen awareness of the fine line between telling a lie and standing in the truth. The common good cracks like a badly plastered wall when falsehood becomes more the norm than the exception. When we express what we believe, we avoid the slippery slope of duplicitous behavior. As a result, evil rumors, idle gossip, erroneous conclusions, and like examples of disingenuous behavior stop before they start.

Integrity reminds us to think before we act. We reflect on our responses while welcoming critique to be sure we have not strayed from the right path. This virtue prompts us to seek the company of like-minded people, who take time in their busy lives to listen to the Lord with open hearts undiluted by preconceived agendas. Our range of listening is both docile and determined, sensitive and responsible, affective and effective. We attune our thoughts and actions to the lasting fruits of integrity we mutually seek. We guard against the tendency to impose our will on others or to strive to control every facet of the situations we share.

Without integrity we may approach relationships as exercises in rugged competition where only the fittest win the prize. With integrity we maintain a vision of life motivated less by the thought of reward and more by a sense of responsibility where what matters most is keeping our word. With the man Job, we say, "till I die I will not put away my integrity from me . . . my heart does not reproach me for any of my days" (Job 27:5–6).

LET US PRAY

Lord, give me the courage to respond in public and in private to what You ask of me. Remind me to listen to Your Word before I speak. Create around me a buffer zone of integrity that frees me from the temptation to look good at the cost of losing my honesty. Let this virtue be and become a non-negotiable trait of my Christian character.

CHAPTER 14
JOY

[E]verlasting joy shall be upon their heads; they shall obtain joy and gladness, and sorrow and sighing shall flee away. (Isaiah 35:10)

Joy is a condition for the possibility of virtuous living. Both momentary joy and lasting joyfulness derive from our receptivity to the transcendent. Joy, together with peace, free us from being too anxious about this or that accomplishment; they ready us to be playful instruments used by God to maintain awe and wonder at the center of our redeemed existence.

This life-giving virtue first reveals itself in the joy we observe in children cared for lovingly by their parents. Their latent powers of formation unfold in playful, spontaneous expressions of sheer delight. They begin to crawl, to walk, to speak those first hesitant words adults love to hear. The joy of performance lights up the child's face with a radiant smile and reminds us as adults how sad it is to lose this original gift.

Despite media reports and their portrayal of a culture of death, we cling to the Apostle Paul's injunction: "Rejoice in the Lord always; again I will say, rejoice" (Philippians 4:4). We must not mistake joy for a superficial bounce into blissful feelings. It is a state of being that prevails through pain and graces us with the capacity to celebrate the peaks and valleys of life. Our daily experiences are not always pleasant. What is no longer gratifying on the vital level of life, nor satisfying on the functional, can still bring us joy in the light of our transcendent presence to the sacred. In that realm all pleasures and displeasures, all satisfactions and dissatisfactions undergo a process of transformation.

We see examples of this curious reversal in the lives of saints and martyrs. In the midst of suffering and mistreatment, they manage to maintain a smile. People admire their witness to the scriptural injunction to rejoice always. This virtue may well be the byproduct of a loving, cheerful, generous heart. The virtue of joy sparks the commitment to remain happy and full of hope despite endless laments about the injustice beheld in the world.

Joy is not a mindless walk in the park but a mindful decision not to engage in useless worry, nor to put our happiness on hold until everything is perfect. Lasting joy leaves an indelible mark on our soul. Consoling feelings of gratification might disappear, but the transcendent quality of joy cannot be erased. This is Jesus' message to His disciples at the close of His earthly life: "Truly, truly, I say to you, you will weep and lament, but the world will rejoice; you will be sorrowful, but your sorrow will turn into joy" (John 16:20).

We fill up with food but feel hungry a little while later. We no sooner achieve one goal then another takes its place. Joy alone has staying power. Joy is more than either of these temporal expressions of gratification or satisfaction. In the midst of everyday demands and the loss of finite possessions like popularity, and all that wealth produces, the joyful choice of life over death, the feeling that every day is worth living, prevails. Alone we might not reach this conclusion, and then we read, "[F]or the joy that was set before him [Christ] endured the cross, despising the shame, and is seated at the right hand of the throne of God" (Hebrews 12:2). His dying and rising was not a cause for weeping but for rejoicing.

At the empty tomb, Jesus asks Mary why she is weeping and tells her to go and tell the disciples that she has seen the Lord (cf. John 20:17). The Easter greeting on the lips of Orthodox believers summarizes the elation we ought to feel: "My joy! Christ is risen." At privileged moments of our faith and formation journey, grace may widen our hearts, filling them to overflowing with a jubilation that surpasses understanding. If we lose this joyfulness, we risk becoming depressed, suicidal people for whom existence holds little or no meaning. We trudge through this world like ants whose only purpose is to advance the army they represent. One ant cannot be distinguished from the next; all follow the same preprogrammed functional line. Such a joyless achievement-only mentality is the ailment of this age. When we reduce who we are to what we do, joy begins to melt away. Our prayer is that we may be infused with the joy-filled wisdom of Jesus, who reminds us of the paradox that a grain of wheat has to die before it yields lasting fruit (cf. John 12:24).

LET US PRAY

Lord, renew in my heart and mind the art and discipline of joyful living in playful intimacy with the Trinity. Implant in me the seeds of joy You have sown in this world. Let the blessings I feel outweigh the burdens life may ask me to carry. Let this surge of radiant joy well up from a heart suffused with the light of Your love. Nothing can stop the joy that overflows my whole being when I contemplate Your presence in and around me. Grant me the grace to cast away the darkness of doubt and restore the inner glow of joyous hope from dawn to the passing of the day.

PART THREE
VIRTUES OF THE SITUATIONAL LIFE

Patience
Perseverance
Wisdom
Contentment
Discipline
Trust
Hope

To live side by side in our family and places of labor and leisure we need the virtues of the situational life. That is where we spend most of our waking hours: in this here-and-now situation, with these people. How well we practice patience, trust, and hope makes all the difference.

CHAPTER 15
PATIENCE

The Lord is not slow about his promise as some count slowness,
but is forbearing toward you, not wishing that any should perish,
but that all should reach repentance. (2 Peter 3:9)

The fruits of the Spirit are "love, joy, peace, patience, kindness, goodness, faithfulness, gentleness, self-control" (Galatians 5:22–23). In this atmosphere of spiritual maturity, patient pondering open to the providence of God prevents us from being tossed to and fro by constant argumentation, discourteous interruptions, and episodes as unimportant as clinging to one's place in line.

Upsurges of impatience may occur when colleagues we planned to meet are not on time or when a domineering type demands the floor. Scenes like this reveal that patience is a hard won virtue. We wish we were more able to wait upon the natural rhythms of life's unfolding but, sad to say, we may not have grown much beyond the volatile impulses of childhood. No matter how old we are, we still lose control, forfeit patient reflection, and fall into reactive patterns that poison an otherwise peaceful atmosphere.

Patience prevents us from running wild. We try to listen lest we lose track of reality. Incidental fads do not easily sway us. Our preference is to assess what we can and cannot do at this moment. Presence to the here-and-now enables us to wait upon further disclosures of grace. Patience relieves us from the relentless pursuit of productivity devoid of peace of mind.

When our best-laid plans go astray, as they often do, patience helps us to avoid hysterical reactions and to learn from the mistakes we've made. It prevents us from killing creativity by aiming arrows of anger at self and others. In receptivity to the Spirit, we choose to handle with the wisdom that comes with experience the imperfections that arise in every situation. We remind ourselves, in the company of saints and sages throughout history, that Rome wasn't built in a day!

While the situation itself may not be changeable at this time, we can change our attitude towards it. Patience allows us to absorb the disappointments we feel when what we longed to achieve does not come to pass, at least not on our timetable. The light may dawn at a later date, but for now we need to trust in divine providence. Progress does not happen under pressure or constraint. The hidden plan of salvation is in no hurry to disclose itself. With infinite patience the Lord holds us and our present circumstances in His timeless embrace.

LET US PRAY

Lord, save me from the pitfalls of impatience and irritability that negate the need to wait upon Your will. Alert me to the paradoxical truth that the perfect script I write may, from the viewpoint of the divine, be a formula for failure. Instead of pushing against the pace of grace and losing my peace, let me accept in every situation what was, is, and will be. Give me the patience to find and follow the plan of life meant for me. Whether You write the text of my destiny in straight or crooked lines, teach me the art and discipline of waiting upon Your mystery—never with clenched fists but always with open hands.

CHAPTER 16
PERSEVERANCE

Therefore, since we are surrounded by so great a cloud of witnesses, let us also lay aside every weight, and sin which clings so closely, and let us run with perseverance the race that is set before us. (Hebrews 12:1)

The temptation to put off until tomorrow what we need to do today is not easy to resist. Procrastination is as powerful a vice as perseverance is a virtue. It wastes energy and complicates our lives. We need to emulate instead Teresa of Avila's practice of "determined determination," which guarantees that a promise made is one that will be kept.

Perseverance curbs deceptive exaltation of what we could do "if only" such and such would happen; it lets us keep a steady eye on what must be done now. We avoid becoming too grave with ourselves and too stern with others. We seek the happy mean between empty hilarity and pushing ourselves too hard because of work not done.

This virtue inspires us to follow the ebb and flow of firmness and gentleness, being stalwart to the end but also taking time to rest and refill our reservoir. Perseverance does not mean plodding through life as if the fate of humanity rested on our shoulders. We do not make our projects the center of the universe by exercising an exaggerated sense of responsibility. We accept problems as challenges and ride the wave of their fulfillment without losing our light-heartedness. Experience has shown us that the more we pray, the more we accomplish, and that good outcomes depend on great faith. We operate from the center of our humility, not from a compulsion to meet the deadlines we've set with no consideration of the divine Will. Prayer is the best partner of perseverance. Participation in this light places us in the presence of God.

Brother Lawrence of the Resurrection, a sixteenth-century Carmelite friar, did not enjoy the blessing of robust health. Although he suffered from severe gout, he was known for his unfailing sense of humor. He did each of his kitchen tasks with such dedication that simply beholding him at work edified others. Soon his reputation for holiness spread beyond the walls of the monastery. So faithfully did he persevere in this style of effortless effort that he became "another Christ" avidly sought by all who longed to see the guidance of God in the givens of their situation.

Whether fulfilling a special assignment or a mundane chore, we remain no more and no less than "tiny pens in a mighty hand." If the saint of Calcutta, Mother Teresa, saw herself as such, who are we to argue with her or Brother Lawrence? Their first course of action was to engage in loving conversations with God.

To foster perseverance in our pursuit of Christian excellence, we need the gift of firmness. To avoid a strident approach fueled by egocentric control that belies God's care, we need the gift of gentleness. The extremes of frantic power-mongering or shallow complacency have no hold over us. Our intention is to stay in touch with God's eternal design and persevere in fulfilling the part we are to play.

LET US PRAY

Lord, I may not always know precisely what You want me to do, but I promise to persevere in Your service without excusing myself from the hardships it may entail. Remind me in whispered inspirations and clear directives of how best to operate in this world. Allow me to avoid emotions like stoic tolerance or pessimistic predictability. Through steadfast prayer open me to the disclosures of Your sacred purpose. Let me persevere in praising Your name while reaffirming my fidelity to do Your will in every situation.

CHAPTER 17
WISDOM

The fear of the Lord is the crown of wisdom, making
peace and perfect health to flourish. (Sirach 1:18)

The virtue of wisdom is like a two-sided coin, combining awe
for the mystery with the tried and tested truths of human and
spiritual experience. Wisdom loosens the tight controls of anxious
achievement and opens the ears of our heart to the music of eternity.
The lucidity of wonder replaces the opaqueness of worldliness.
Wisdom brightens the shadows of our life and lets us commune with
the nimble, translucent vision of Trinitarian love revealed to us. The
words of Solomon never fail to inspire a waning soul:

> For in her there is a spirit that is intelligent, holy,
> unique, manifold, subtle,
> mobile, clear, unpolluted,
> distinct, invulnerable, loving the good, keen,
> irresistible, beneficent, humane,
> steadfast, sure, free from anxiety,
> all-powerful, overseeing all,
> and penetrating through all spirits
> that are intelligent and pure and most subtle.
> For wisdom is more mobile than any motion;
> because of her pureness she pervades and penetrates all
> things.

For she is a breath of the power of God,
and a pure emanation of the glory of the Almighty.
(Wisdom 7:22–25)

Insofar as foolish thoughts distract our attention, we can rely on wisdom to return us to our center in God. Rather than being pressured by outside influences, and complaining until we get our way, we root our decisions and actions in faith and reason, the two wings of truth. What holds our attention are "the secret purposes of God" (Wisdom 2:22) since, thanks to this seminal virtue, we have grown beyond childish displays of disappointed pouting when the plans we proposed fall apart.

This gift gains in power when we place ourselves under the care of good teachers endowed at whatever age with the insight and experience for which we all pray. St. Thérèse of Lisieux died when she was only twenty-four, but her works were found to be so full of wisdom that she was declared a doctor of the Church. To the smallest situation, be it folding the sisters' mantles, pushing an elderly nun in a wheelchair, or practicing the ministry of the smile when she had the strength for nothing else, she brought a wealth of wisdom to her "little way or spiritual childhood," and conveyed by her example the efficacy of inhaling and exhaling the breath of God.[1]

With the passage of years, we may experience an increase in wisdom by putting aside our selfish ways and adhering to the constellation of virtues that circle around it, including self-control, prudence, justice, and courage (cf. Wisdom 8:7). In the company of like-minded companions and in accordance with the gifts and talents we share, new avenues of service open before us. We beseech the Spirit to renew our personal lives and to guide our efforts to transform the world into the house of God.

---

1 See *The Autobiography of St. Thérèse of Lisieux*, trans. John Clarke (Washington, DC: ICS Publications, 1975), Chapter 8, 167.

LET US PRAY

Lord, deliver me from egocentric ways of control that veil wisdom. Protect me from whatever obscures the light of the truth. Remind me that mere learning is not enough to evoke the gift of wisdom. In Your mercy, draw me into the epicenter of this virtue, allowing me to lodge myself in her "house of instruction" (Sirach 51:23, NAB).

CHAPTER 18

CONTENTMENT

There is great gain in godliness with contentment;
for we brought nothing into the world, and we cannot
take anything out of the world; but if we have food and
clothing, with these we shall be content. (1 Timothy 6: 6–8)

The current running through many situations at home and in the marketplace is more one of discontent than of contentment. The air bristles with curt answers, harsh critique, and a lack of cordiality. The hype surrounding mere consumerism tries to convince us that we can fill the hole in our heart with more possessions than we need. We shop and shop and still feel empty. Avarice obliterates generosity. Greed grinds regular sharing to a halt. The pressure to gain more brings functioning to a frantic pace with no time spent in Sabbath rest. The question of who owns what takes precedence over the consonance of living in a Christian community where people share and share alike.

Scenes characterized by infighting take us far away from the serene shores of a contented life where the good of one extends beyond the boundary of wealth or want to enhance the good of all. Opposing factions feel free to voice their concerns without forfeiting the possibility of reaching as much consensus as possible. The undercurrent of contentment inspires us to go beyond the tensions created by a cacophony of warring voices until we come to a workable resolution that benefits all factions.

The virtue of contentment allows for a coincidence of opposites: likes-dislikes; successes-failures; losses-gains. It teaches us the art of integrating the functional and the transcendent. Our starting point is to accept whatever His holy providence sends our way instead of being driven only by motives distorted by power, pleasure, and possession.

Progress in private and public life is more likely to be ours when we are "content with little or much" (Sirach 29:23). Virtue, not vice, becomes our chief character trait when we are "for the sake of Christ . . . content with weaknesses, insults, hardships, persecutions, and calamities; for when I am weak, then I am strong" (2 Corinthians 12:10).

Would not the world be a better place were we to be content with whatever we have (cf. Philippians 4:11)? The Apostle Paul taught this secret to those newly converted to Christ: "I know how to be abased, and I know how to abound; in any and all circumstances I have learned the secret of facing plenty and hunger, abundance and want. I can do all things in him who strengthens me" (Philippians 4:12–13).

These and other biblical counsels to be content with what we have (cf. Hebrews 13:5) create a sense of serenity in our heart and a climate of equanimity in our life as a whole. Such gifts are not mastered by us but bestowed upon us; they are not the effect of rigorous, regimented labors but an outflow of divinely inspired peace and joy.

Contentment is not quiescence; there is no inclination in us to escape what is unpleasant or to draw battle lines unamenable to reconciliation. We rise above the extremes of complacency or bellicosity. We prefer to assess the situation as it is while meeting with prudence, justice, fortitude, and temperance the challenges placed before us. When someone needs us, we lay aside our plans. When life demands action, we suspend our fear of failure. When we forget to live in fidelity, we face our guilt and seek forgiveness. When we lose our way, we remember with a humble, contented smile, the many times God has held our hand and brought us home.

Think of the contentment felt by the centurion when he returned to his house and found his servant in good health (cf. Luke 7:1–10). Could we imagine a more serene visage than that of the woman caught in adultery and saved by Jesus from stoning on the condition that from then on she does not sin again (cf. John 8:1–11). Many other discontented souls are returned to contented harmony by the Lord. When such out-of-sort disruptions invade our being, there is no use denying them. The way to attain a life of harmony is to see in every happening an opportunity to walk in the footsteps of the Lord.

LET US PRAY

Lord, help me to move from the self-imposed pressure of meeting so many obligations to the port of inner and outer equanimity. Teach me to emulate the gracious manner in which You moved from dining with sinners to discussing weighty matters with scholars. Contentment comes when I live in the gentle rhythm of relaxed presence and firm resolve, of resting in You and then resuming my work. With the psalmist, let me be content in knowing that "goodness and mercy shall follow me all the days of my life; and I shall dwell in the house of the Lord for ever" (Psalm 23:6).

CHAPTER 19
DISCIPLINE

Having been disciplined a little, they will receive great good, because God tested them and found them worthy of himself. (Wisdom 3:5)

The virtue of discipline is the first fruit of discipleship. It is impossible to imagine ourselves making "disciples of all nations" (Matthew 28:19) without adhering to the practices Jesus taught us. The primary discipline He gave us was to love one another as He loved us (cf. John 13:34–35). If we do not obey this command, we may be tempted to ignore the blessings and shrink from the burdens of charitable discipleship. We may boast of the good we do to gain fame and broadcast our achievements. The discipline of self-forgetful love may succumb to the detour of selfish sensuality. In our rush to climb the ladder of corporate control, we forget what it means to be followers of Jesus in spirit and truth. The Apostle James voiced his concern in this regard saying, "So faith by itself, if it has no works, is dead" (James 2:17).

Rather than associate discipline with harsh methods of mortification, we ought to foster a master-disciple relationship, rooted in our willingness to obey the Word of the Lord. No commission we receive can be fulfilled unless we link this discipline with discipleship:

> It is for discipline that you have to endure. God is treating you as sons; for what son is there whom his

father does not discipline? If you are left without discipline, in which all have participated, then you are illegitimate children and not sons. Besides this, we have had earthly fathers to discipline us and we respected them. Shall we not much more be subject to the Father of spirits and live? (Hebrews 12:7–9)

The Letter to the Hebrews goes on to explain that our parents discipline us at the right time and in accordance with what they deem best for the family unit. God disciplines us for our own good so that we may share in the life of holiness that signifies our covenant of friendship. The discipline asked of us may often seem more painful than pleasant, but "later it yields the peaceful fruit of righteousness to those who have been trained by it" (Hebrews 12:11).

An exemplary discipline emblazoned on the hearts of servants of the Lord is obedience. Because He has chosen us to live by and witness to His Word, despite our limitations, we beg for the grace to listen. Because the Almighty has bestowed such a great favor upon us, we feel empowered to stand up for what is right in every situation without falling prey to either anxiety or ego-exaltation. What we do is not merely another duty to be accomplished in a long string of endless projects; it is a way of seeing every endeavor assigned to us by God as another chapter in the book of discipleship. The disciplines we embrace, from spiritual reading to serving our neighbor, stem from the desire to be and become better listeners to the Gospel directives we have received.

The Apostle Peter reminds us that disciples and friends of God must remain vigilant because "Your adversary the devil prowls around like a roaring lion, seeking some one to devour" (1 Peter 5:8). Reading God's Word and meditating upon it, praying unceasingly and practicing charity, are spiritual exercises that ready us to resist demonic seduction and advance the reign of God on earth.

LET US PRAY

Lord, lead me away from the trap of superficial piety devoid of care for others. Grant me a small portion of the truth known to all saintly people that other-centered love is the chief discipline of discipleship. In response to Your grace, let me become Your servant in this world without becoming its slave. Take me with You into the desert of discipline that I may be found worthy to be sent forth into this world as an ambassador of Your mystery (cf. 2 Corinthians 5:20).

CHAPTER 20

TRUST

*Those who trust in him will understand truth, and the faithful will
abide with him in love, because grace and mercy are upon his elect,
and he watches over his holy ones. (Wisdom 3:9)*

It appears as if we break out of the throes of complacency and
become more open to the grace of character formation in Christ
when a crisis tests our endurance. Our only choice is to trust, without
reservation, that there will be light at the end of this tunnel.

To trust or not to trust in Love divine is a basic option each of us
must make. That first inch of relinquishment may lead to an habitual
disposition of yielding, but this grace exacts the price of our having
to give up any illusion of ultimate control. Reliance on our own
willfulness becomes ludicrous. As wanderers long to find an oasis in
the arid deserts they have to cross, so we desire a resurgence of trust in
God to sustain us from day to day. Such dependence is not a sign of
weakness but the source of our well-being.

For every ounce of discouragement that weighs us down, we
need to gain an extra pound of trust. Whenever doubts proliferate in
our minds, we must stop these convoluted reasoning processes and
concentrate instead on the cornerstone of trust in Christ, who said,
"I will not leave you desolate" (John 14:18). To trust is to follow the
Good Shepherd and say to Him, "Even though I walk through the
valley of the shadow of death, I fear no evil; for thou art with me; thy
rod and thy staff, they comfort me" (Psalm 23:4).

A trustful attitude leads us to acknowledge the immensity of God's fidelity to us. Instead of forcing our solution upon every situation, we remain open to the Spirit's communication of God's plan through apparently unconnected circumstances. In this way we go beyond the assumption that unwanted events have no meaning and trust the truth that God's ways, though not our own, will one day be revealed to us in all their grace and glory.

Understandably, we feel disappointed when a dream of ours does not come true, but at such moments we say as soon as possible, "Behold, God is my salvation; I will trust, and will not be afraid" (Isaiah 12:2). The trust that God will not fail us helps us to get through whatever happens, from a fractured relationship to the fear of our own finitude. In the tightest predicament we feel sure that God will rush to our aid in one way or another.

Trust is our anchor in the turbulent ocean of an untrusting world. This virtue transports us from despair to hope. We know that the Lord may test us in times of trial but not beyond our strength to endure. Trust frees us from the dead-end streets of fear and suspicion and opens us to fresh vistas of hope and blessed assurance. It lets us see the drudgery of the day in a new light. It gives meaning to the most mundane endeavors. What we do becomes a litany of praise to the divine Presence permeating all that is. The simplest tasks glow with epiphanic radiance when trust reigns in our heart.

Christ asks us to remain like little children who trust their parents and at no moment doubt their protection. And yet, before we know it, our aggressive, doubt-ridden defenses threaten to break down the reliable walls of this virtue. To fail in trust once in a while ought to be no cause for alarm. We are, after all, fallen in our humanity. Christ sees our good will, though our actions may at times declare the contrary. What matters is that we try to trust and let God judge the efficacy of our surrender. The gift of trust may then enter into the deepest recesses of our being, though on the surface of life we may still feel the turmoil of doubt. When our burdens become too much to bear, we lay them at Christ's feet and say, "Jesus, I trust in you." We put aside what seems impossible to us and exercise the conviction that all things are possible for Him (cf. Luke 1:37).

LET US PRAY

Lord, in the nights that test my trust, may Your promise of fidelity sustain me. At moments when, humanly speaking, You seem farthest away, let my trust in You assure me that You are most near. In appreciative abandonment to Your mystery, let me entrust my whole being, from birth to death, to You. Let this gift of surrender be the mark of my complete conversion to the form of Christ hidden in my soul. Amidst doubters and naysayers, let me proclaim, "I will put my trust in him" (Hebrews 2:13).

CHAPTER 21

HOPE

Trust in him, and he will help you; make your ways straight,
and hope in him. (Sirach 2:6)

Hope is a virtue none of us can live without. In countless situations
in which we find ourselves, we have to cope with pinpricks of
disappointment and near despair. A person we trusted speaks ill of
us to the boss. An investment we made in good faith puts money
in another's pocket. The mechanic who promised to repair our car
does a shoddy job. Each time our hope takes another battering we are
tempted to throw in the towel. And yet this infused virtue pushes its
way through the gritty nets of depreciative living and comes to our
rescue. Once more we decide to hope against hope. We choose to
believe that after midnight comes the dawn. No sooner do we place
our hope not in human frailty but in the Lord than we learn that
"hope does not disappoint us" (Romans 5:5).

Paradoxically, the test of hope is hopelessness. According to G.K.
Chesterton, "Hope means hoping when things are hopeless, or it is
no virtue at all. . . . As long as matters are really hopeful, hope is
mere flattery or platitude; it is only when everything is hopeless that
hope begins to be a strength."[1] After being downsized, a person may
have few prospects for the future, but still he or she dresses up and
hits the pavement, determined to find employment. Hope counters

---

1 G.K. Chesterton, *Heretics* (London: John Lane, 1952), 119

uncertainty and fear. It keeps us from becoming complacent. It represents for believers an act of supreme confidence in Christ, the "hope of glory" (Colossians 1:27).

Hope counteracts the narcissistic expectation that life has to follow our script and guarantee gratification. With hopeful hearts we can face the harshness of reality without giving up. Hope lives on when there are no miracles being performed and no consolations felt. It will not permit us to sink into scornful pessimism. We do not hope in the possible, which may be under human control, but in the impossible, which falls under the providential design of God.

Hope is inherently paradoxical. It explains why, when life reaches its lowest point, we get up and start over again. It prompts us to ask for help by rejecting the lie that we can save ourselves. It counteracts the narcissistic conclusion that life is not worth living when our expectations are not met. In contrast to hopelessness, resignation, or pessimistic acceptance of a predetermined fate, hope anticipates the surprises of God. To wrestle with angelic hosts as Jacob did (cf. Genesis 32:22–32), to bargain with God to save the city if only a handful of faithful can be found, as Abraham did (cf. Genesis 18:16–32), is to live in hope.

Hope does not depend on accurate prediction or problem solving but on presence to the unfolding of God's will in ways known and unknown in daily life. Hope tells us to dream our dreams while reminding us that only with God's help can we put firm and lasting foundations under them.

Three conditions facilitate our formation in hope. The first is to wait upon the mystery with utmost confidence that a course of action providing relief from the feeling of being abandoned will be revealed. We believe that the hour will come when God will shatter the silence and speak to our waiting hearts a word of hope.

The second is continual conversation with God, especially during those trying times of life that by human standards appear to be the antithesis of hope. This theological virtue readies us to receive lights we can neither predict nor imagine nor fully understand except for the fact that we know that God will turn these switches on one day soon.

The third is to behold in the richness of the ordinary how the Spirit responds to our cry for the renewal of hope. When we consecrate our lives in and with Christ to the Father, then the bread of responsibility and the wine of sensitivity are transformed into a thanksgiving sacrifice. We find in everyday life new reasons to leave our hopeless churnings behind and place our past, present, and future wholly in God's hands.

LET US PRAY

Lord, when I feel low in spirit, whisper a word of hope that generates certitude in my uncertain heart. Open portals of hope that encourage me to view life through a brighter lens. Let hope be the doorway I pass through to a transformed life that reveals the value of redemptive suffering. Teach me to let go of my locked-in agendas and turn to You. Empty my memory of past hurts and disappointments. Cleanse my imagination of plans and expectations for which there is no guarantee. Break the bonds of despair that hold me captive. Transform the dying embers of hopelessness into the roaring fires of fully hopeful living.

PART FOUR
VIRTUES OF THE GLOBAL LIFE

Generosity
Justice
Liberty
Loyalty
Zeal
Thanksgiving
Serenity

To increase the awareness that we are not alone, that we share life on Planet Earth, is to strive for such global virtues as generosity, justice, and peace. The world will be and become a "space of grace" to the degree that virtue replaces vice.

CHAPTER 22

GENEROSITY

Every good endowment and every perfect gift is from above,
coming down from the Father of lights with whom there is
no variation or shadow due to change. (James 1:17)

Sayings from the Gospel like "Render therefore to Caesar the things that are Caesar's, and to God the things that are God's" (Matthew 22:21) are without ambiguity. The Pharisees tried to trap Jesus over the issue of paying taxes but the minted coins they held told them precisely what to do. Other passages demand much more pondering. Jesus makes clear that lamplight ought not to be hid under a bushel basket (cf. Mark 4:21–22); He then appeals to His listeners to open their ears to what living the virtue of generosity really demands: "[T]he measure you give will be the measure you get, and still more will be given you. For to him who has will more be given; and from him who has not, even what he has will be taken away" (Mark 4:24–25).

What Jesus seems to be saying is this: the more generous we are, the more we will receive, for God is a generous giver. Sadly, those who pretend to have nothing—not so much as one coin—even that will be taken from them. The Lord has no tolerance for greed. In this scathing condemnation of the hypocritical scribes and Pharisees, He warns, "for you cleanse the outside of the cup and of the plate, but inside they are full of extortion and rapacity" (Matthew 23:25).

The financial scandals that have rocked our world ought to be enough to convince us how heartless this vice is. According to

Scripture, it puts us in the company of "drunkards," "revilers," and "robbers" (1 Corinthians 6:10); it "stirs up strife" (Proverbs 28:25); and, worst of all, it places before any other good that of personal gain only. Little wonder the Apostle Paul compares it to idolatry (cf. Colossians 3:5).

The tentacles of greed may wrap themselves around us as early as childhood. Consider so-called childish pranks like candy swiping or pilfering another student's homework. Are these merely naughty acts or might they pave the way for greater evils? Unchecked in our youth, sinful habits like stealing may have degenerative effects on character development. It becomes "no big deal" to take what does not belong to us and feel neither remorse nor the obligation to make restitution. Yet, as experience verifies, as goes the child, so goes the adult.

The only virtue strong enough to counteract vices rooted in greed is generosity, which represents a major shift from ownership to stewardship. We give as much from our surplus as from our want; we offer material help like money and spiritual gifts like our time. We loosen the grip of greed as often as we can because we know we owe everything to God. The reaches of generosity are so wide that they include as their fruits joy, peace, patience, and kindness (cf. Galatians 5:22).

In a space divided along strict lines of the "haves" and "have nots," everyone loses. When the rich become richer by breaking the backs of the poor, both segments of the population suffer. Only one act of unprecedented generosity could counter the cruel effects of avarice: the Son of God had to become poor for our sake (cf. 2 Corinthians 8:9) so that we could shun selfishness, loosen the grip of greed, and pass on to others what we cannot take with us anyway: "For what will it profit a man, if he gains the whole world but forfeits his life?" (Matthew 16:26).

The answer to this question ought to change our tune. If we do not cooperate with the grace God has given us by being gracious to others, greed will gnaw away at charity's heel like a hungry dog. On that bone will be left no meat of compassion to feed the hungry and shelter the homeless. In a culture that fosters acquisition-at-any-cost, that equates wealth with happiness and sees possessions as status symbols, it is tempting to amass so many things that they soon possess us. The irony is that goods originally given to us by God can be the cause of our separation from God.

Collections of quantifiable goods do not necessarily form good character traits. How we handle them is what counts. Our formation in Christ comes to fruition when we keep our eyes on who people are, not on what they own. We value our original worth in God and try to jump over the fence greedy inclinations erect between us. Greed isolates us from others; generosity prompts us to celebrate our mutual togetherness in the family of the Trinity. We know where our treasure is (cf. Matthew 6:21). When moths bore holes in our stockpiles of material goods, they teach us that lasting happiness is not to be found in households overcrowded with this and that but in the God who made them.

LET US PRAY

Lord, each time avarice tempts me to hold on to what is not mine, let these generous words of Job be on my lips: "[N]aked I came from my mother's womb, and naked shall I return; the LORD gave, and the LORD has taken away; blessed be the name of LORD" (Job 1:21). Help me individually and all of us collectively to banish greed and its gross effects on the innocents of this world. By Your grace may we become living examples of the true wealth that is ours when we exercise the enduring virtue of generosity.

CHAPTER 23
JUSTICE

But let justice roll down like waters, and
righteousness like an everflowing stream. (Amos 5:24)

Justice is a unique moral virtue with universal implications. Its root is the constant and firm will to treat every person with equal dignity before the Lord and to give them their due over the span of a lifetime in an atmosphere of freedom and responsibility.

To practice justice is to respect the personal, civil, and social rights of all people; it is to uphold the worth of every citizen from conception to natural death with a willingness to protect the most vulnerable. Justice enables us to do what it takes to promote fair and balanced relationships and to bolster the conditions necessary for fostering the common good. When just women and men do their duty in a democratic society, they make sure that every person in their country, themselves included, respect property rights, pay their debts, and fulfill contractual obligations. They monitor what the community owes to others and what is owed to them. Parents show respect for adult children when they uphold their right to make their own life choices. Children respect their parents when they take into account their advice and try, should they disagree, to exercise restraint and explain as clearly as possible their decisions.

This basic right to life, liberty, and the pursuit of happiness comes under attack whenever we ignore or suppress the truth that we are created, redeemed, and sanctified by God. Our obligation is to respect one another regardless of our race, color, creed, or culture of origin. Lacking this climate of social justice, real dialogue is likely to come to a halt. Individuals as well as whole groups of people may succumb to the detrimental effects of oppression, discrimination, and unjust persecution. Wounds as deep as these must be commended to God for healing. As the prophet says, "He will not fail or be discouraged till he has established justice in the earth; and the coastlands wait for his law" (Isaiah 42:4).

The malady of social injustice, perpetrated by ruthless individuals or oppressive regimes, leads to acts of tyranny that threaten to destroy the very fabric of society. Such gross violations of human rights make people feel as if they are mere pawns on a game board pushed hither and yon, used and abused for others' gain. Justice upholds the truth that all people under God are entitled to basic goods like food, clothing, and shelter. Injustice perpetrates the lie that only a privileged few ought to have access to the earth's resources. Around them usually swirl the ill winds of tyranny, extortion, gang violence, and crimes so heinous they may be punishable by life in prison.

Followers of Christ refuse to condone the treachery injustice breeds. They consider their needs secondary to those of their neighbor. Paradoxically, the unjust mentality that strikes a blow at discipleship may become the seedbed of myriad expressions of just and equitable treatment. Advocates of social justice curb the suffering cruel tyrants inflict on their sisters and brothers. They take whatever steps are necessary to create a society that neglects no one and conducts its affairs with justice (cf. Psalm 112:5).

One cautionary note is in order here: personal justice is not immune from the pressures of social injustice. For instance, a school official may bolster the grade of an undeserving student, fearful that his or her parents may withhold their yearly donation. Mistaken notions of what constitutes justice may be mingled with the excuse that the student in question needs to feel affirmed and encouraged and to start a successful career. The official forgets that this dishonest beginning is an act of social injustice. To send an unqualified person into society as a trustworthy professional will neither help future clients nor advance the spiritual formation of the overly protected person.

A similar case involves parents who refuse to discipline a child reasonably yet firmly. Misguided by a warped sense of compassion, they prepare the ground for the injustice to society this child may perpetrate as a spoiled adult who threatens others when his or her demands are not met. Parents may try to appease children who are not dedicated to their chores or who are disrespectful of their teachers. To spare themselves the burden of discipline, they may indulge a child's lack of zeal and engagement under the pretext of extending to him or her their just due. By allowing children to be careless, habitually depreciative, and demanding of attention, they risk impoverishing in some measure not only the youngster in question but also the fabric of society itself.

When power politics prevail in institutions like colleges, hospitals, or humanitarian organizations, injustices may follow. Administrators may be moved in their actions by such unjust dispositions as how to look good in the eyes of the public or how to be effective professionally while protecting and advancing one's own social position. The upsurge of power politics appears to be a given in the human condition. The blindness occasioned by unjustly exalting oneself has to be dealt with by those invested with legitimate authority and subjected always to the power of prayer.

LET US PRAY

Lord, erase from my soul the demeaning dispositions of disrespect and indifference that threaten to crush life in family, Church, and society. Grant me the grace of extending to persons near and far the virtues of social justice, peace, and mercy. Let me do what I can to prevent the spread of violence at home and abroad and to confront injustice wherever it is found. Never let me be contaminated by an anti-Christian climate that depreciates one segment of society for the sake of promoting the dominance of another. May I, together with others, find creative ways to appraise our faults and renew our commitment to defend equality in dignity since "When justice is done, it is a joy to the righteous, but dismay to evildoers" (Proverbs 21:15).

CHAPTER 23
LIBERTY

> The Spirit of the Lord God is upon me, because the Lord
> has anointed me to bring good tidings to the afflicted; he has
> sent me to bind up the brokenhearted, to proclaim liberty to the
> captives, and the opening of the prison to those who are bound;
> to proclaim the year of the Lord's favor. (Isaiah 61:1–2)

Liberty is not license. It is a longing placed by God in every human heart. All of us want to be freed from the chains that bind us to vices like avarice and gluttony, lust and anger. This prophetic declaration of Isaiah beckons us to leave behind the illusions that entrap us so that we can journey with a lighter load to the promised land. The letdowns that occur when we let go of the attachments that feign freedom are as painful as they are illuminating.

Nothing less than God can satisfy the restless longings in our heart. Plans go astray. Outcomes remain unmet. Self-confidence erodes. Times like these may be the passageways grace uses to release us from the imprisoning power of excessive security directives. Only when we see beyond these sad substitutes for the transcendent is it possible for us to make a fresh start. Attachments this intense never loosen their grip if we assume a posture of self-pity, blame others for our troubles, and argue that they, not we, have a problem. We fail to realize that our cravings for lesser goods are like yapping dogs that have to be fed. Even after eating they never stop barking.

Inordinate attachments paralyze flexible, Spirit-illumined freedoms. They narrow the window through which we view life. We may not be able to remember the last time we enjoyed sunrises and sunsets, conversations with friends over a relaxing meal or days not dominated by stressful consumerism. When we try to outdo others at the expense of their and our integrity, we end up drained of physical and spiritual energy. We fail to see in honesty and humility the fuller picture of our purpose on earth.

What liberates us at the deepest level is our adherence to the truths revealed to us by the freeing power of God's Word. We find in the Bible that the path to intimacy with the triune God can only be traversed when love prevails over hate, when peace replaces war, when forgiveness overcomes revenge. What causes us to rejoice is that we are "not being without law toward God but under the law of Christ" (1 Corinthians 9:21). So liberated by this law of love is the Apostle Paul that he has become under the impetus of grace "all things to all men, that [he] might by all means save some" (1 Corinthians 9:22).

Having been freed from our sins by the blood of Christ, having been justified not by our works but by our faith in Him, we are free to pursue the new covenant of love and liberation He initiated, for where His spirit is, there freedom itself is to be found (cf. 2 Corinthians 3:17). The same Lord who sets us free from the bondage of sin commands us not to use our freedom "as a pretext for evil" (1 Peter 2:16). The more we make of our whole self a free offering to the Lord, the happier we will be. Unfree people often resort to lawlessness to advance their nefarious causes; free people live within the law given to them through Moses while recognizing in Christ that they are not under the law: "For you were called to freedom, brethren; only do not use your freedom as an opportunity for the flesh, but through love be servants of one another" (Galatians 5:13).

Dispelled when we follow the Lord are the shadows of despondency and false guilt that discourage us from pursuing the freedom of the children of God (cf. Romans 8:14–17). The Lord reminds us that despite our human faults and failings we are loved by Him into a freer way of being and doing. In the same vein, the masters of Christian formation—ancient, medieval, and modern—never tire of telling us of the need to form, reform, and transform our lives in conformity to Christ. They gather together the foundations of transcendent living found in Holy Scripture and many different schools of spirituality and show us what they have in common. All proclaim the freedom of the children of God whose first duty is to imbibe the cumulative wisdom of Christian living. It sheds light on the liberating course set for us by the Holy Spirit and helps us to fulfill our destiny.

LET US PRAY

Lord, when I feel entrapped in prisons of my own making, remind me of Your promise of liberty. Loosen the bonds of sin that strangle the freedom found in obedience to You. Let my quest for liberty be linked to the divine directives communicated to me. Whenever I forfeit my freedom due to disobedience, grant me the grace of forgiveness. Let me dwell no longer on what stunts my spiritual growth but on what advances my flight to You in adversity and prosperity, in desolation and consolation. Let me be free enough to see in every cloud a silver lining, in every call to renunciation another key to liberation.

CHAPTER 23
LOYALTY

Know . . . that the Lord your God is God, the faithful God who keeps covenant and steadfast love with those who love him and keep his commandments, to a thousand generations. (Deuteronomy 7:9)

The words of the Gospel are so laden with meaning that they invite continual reflection on what we have heard and read. We must dive beneath their surface significance to discover what is applicable to the unfolding of our own call, vocation, and avocation. These sacred utterances are carriers of hidden wisdom. They stir the heart of every receptive listener. They point to the impenetrable depths of divine transformation. They remind us that no amount of faith formation can bring our search to closure. We pass through pockets of light between long stretches of darkness.

The Spirit makes us grow more by faith than by sight. Each successive opening becomes an opportunity to articulate what our everyday life in family, Church, and society means in dialogue with the words of everlasting life disclosed to us with the assistance of the Spirit. The vast sea of this Revelation can never be poured in its mysterious totality into the narrow channels of our created minds. With or without understanding, all we can hope to say is that "I have fought the good fight, I have finished the race, I have kept the faith" (2 Timothy 4:7).

The ode to a capable wife in the Book of Proverbs (31:10–31) offers an unforgettable description of this virtue of loyalty. She evokes trust, does no harm, provides food for her household, opens her hands to the poor, manifests strength and dignity, does not eat the bread of idleness, and fears the Lord. Like a loyal friend, she is a joy forever. Here is one on whom we can rely, who will stand by us through thick and thin, one who will chart a steady course by working for our good both in our presence and in our absence (cf. Matthew 24:45–46).

Loyalty of this sort lessens the sting of betrayal we may have felt at one time or another. It silences our fear that fewer and fewer people in public and private life are to be trusted. Loyalty assures us that fidelity will prevail over falsehood and that friends like this are among the greatest gifts of God. It would be inconceivable for them to be disloyal in the face of vexing problems or tedious tasks. The support they offer is freely given and never fickle. Their word is golden; the veracity of their promises erases our doubts. Such loyalty is neither dependent on the level of one's education nor on worldly standards of success like charm and cleverness. These attributes are no guarantee that a person will be loyal to us. What we like most are not appearances but generous hearts, not smooth talkers but trustworthy confidants.

Loyalty is like an eternal flame. Once enkindled by grace, it cannot be extinguished. It exudes a steady stream of reliability without fanfare or affectation. A loyal companion has no need to ruffle the feathers of egocentric control. If we fall down, he or she lifts us up; if we fail, kind words encourage us to try again. Whereas disloyalty leaves us feeling empty and perplexed, loyalty renews our strength and restores our faith in humankind.

In a swirling sea of individualistic competition, where we feel battered by duplicity and disloyalty, we need a steadfast rock to cling to. Every expression of loyalty we receive shows us that gains in grace outweigh the losses caused by vice. In the simplest of acts—a meal selflessly prepared and served; a phone call made at the exact moment we feel most alone; a repair so well done that an appliance we were about to discard can be used again—we know from experience that "the people who know their God shall stand firm and take action" (Daniel 11:32). The world will be a better place because of them.

LET US PRAY

Lord, never let me doubt that my loyalty to You is but a dim reflection of Your loyalty to me. I marvel that despite the betrayal inflicted upon You, nothing deterred You from the course set for You by the Father. May this virtue help me to stand firm in the face of disloyalty; may it remind me that You are the lamp that never stops shining, for "With the loyal, you show yourself loyal; with the blameless man you show yourself blameless" (2 Samuel 22:26).

CHAPTER 26
ZEAL

"Take these things away; you shall not make my Father's
house a house of trade." His disciples remembered that it was
written, "Zeal for your house will consume me." (John 2:16–17)

This virtue signifies the love of God in action; it enables us to maintain fervent adherence to what we know to be a true and righteous endeavor; it promotes the ardor we need to uphold our commitment to a cause we champion. Zeal aids the embodiment of such Christian formation ideals as that embodied in the Golden Rule: "As you wish that men would do to you, do so to them" (Luke 6:31). Zealous persons can complete a task as out of the ordinary as funding a capital campaign to rebuild their church or as ordinary as delivering meals to elderly shut-ins in their congregation.

Zeal lets us shine with a double dose of charity—love of God and of neighbor. It prompts us not to rest on what we have attained, thanks to the grace of God, but to request our next assignment. The shadow side of zeal can result in our becoming a zealot or a fanatic of some sort, usually religious or political, but behavior like this is a vice, not a virtue. True zeal draws us, in the words of the psalmist, to "love righteousness and hate wickedness" (Psalm 45:7).

The fire of holiness enkindled in us by the grace of God fuels zeal. We become devoted to prayer and desirous of gaining a more intimate knowledge of God. We find devotion sweet and discipline a delight. We want everyone, ourselves included, to embrace the Cross with joy and to see in suffering the chance to identify with Christ's own crucifying epiphany.

Zeal motivates us to imitate the love-will of the Son to the Father. It is incumbent upon us to lead others to the path of salvation and not to grow slack in this intention. As Jesus gave Himself tirelessly to redeem us, so we want to empty ourselves of every trace of egocentricity and wash others' feet.

Zeal deepens our sensitivity to missing the mark—to waywardness and willful sin. These offenses do not cause us to despair of God's forgiveness; they remind us with what zeal the Good Shepherd left the ninety-nine behind to seek the one lamb lost in the wilderness (cf. Luke 15:3–7). Faithfulness thus freely bestowed increases our fervor and offers us the incentive we need not to break any commandment of God or the Church.

In this virtue we find the antidote to sloth, a buffer zone to protect us from the onslaught of disobedience, dejection, and listlessness. Individually and as a community, this virtue strengthens our faith and teaches us who to befriend and what to avoid. The zealous souls of parents and teachers are models for us of devotionality, charitable acts, and empathetic dispositions. Zeal guards our heart from temptations and prevents tepidity. It encourages us to keep our inner house in order and to do something daily to make spiritual progress. It prompts us to work above and beyond the call of duty and to shun any form of scandalous misbehavior.

Those zealous to serve the Lord welcome course-corrective admonishments as well as assurances that the road they are on is the right one. When luke-warmness threatens to invade the citadel of fervent faith, it is not strange that zeal for God's house consumes them (cf. Psalm 69:9) with a sense of mission and ministry the enemy can never defeat.

LET US PRAY

Lord, may my zeal not grow tame or tempted by idleness nor may my fervor be dissipated in erratic choices severed from Your will. Never let fanaticism sway me from the truths You have revealed. With the zeal of the Lord of hosts to accomplish His work in me (Isaiah 37:32), I believe I can meet the challenges set before me while attributing to You the power to "put false ways far from me" (Psalm 119:29) and to grant me the grace to "meditate on your wondrous works" (Psalm 119:27).

CHAPTER 27

THANKSGIVING

The Lord is at hand. Have no anxiety about anything, but
in everything by prayer and supplication with thanksgiving
let your requests be made known to God. (Philippians 4:5–6)

Global awareness of the wondrous resources we must never take
for granted parallels expressions of thanksgiving that accompany
and increase our ecological sensitivity. In creation we behold the first
revelation of the Lord. We are no less awed by the infinite reaches
of the cosmos than we are by the minute cellular units in our body.
Realizing how fearfully and wonderfully made we and all of God's
works are, we pray with the psalmist:

> I give you thanks, O LORD, with my whole heart;
>   before the angels I sing your praise;
> I bow down toward your holy temple
>   and give thanks to your name for your mercy and
> your faithfulness;
> for you have exalted above everything
>   your name and your word. (Psalm 138:1–2)

In days of old, worshipers brought before the Lord "sacrifices and
thank offerings" (2 Chronicles 29:31), but this practice need not be
confined to the ancients. Can we not make a thank offering for the
unpolluting of the air, for the good stewardship of the globe, for the
variety of fruits and vegetables lavishly spread on our table?

Thankfulness is a virtue that demands daily nurturing. Are we so indifferent, so lacking in insight, that we fail to thank God for the boundless blessings we receive. The results of failing to make these thank offerings are documented in Paul's letter to the Romans: "So they are without excuse; for although they knew God they did not honor him as God or give thanks to him, but they became futile in their thinking and their senseless minds were darkened" (Romans 1:20–21).

Instead of bowing in gratitude to God, we foolish humans built idols subject to destruction. Only the saving power of the divine could return us to the praise that wells up spontaneously from a humble and grateful heart, obedient to the Gospel and generous in sharing with others "because of the surpassing grace of God in [us]" (2 Corinthians 9:14). Our response has to be in kind. Day and night we acknowledge how holy God is. We "give glory and honor and thanks to him who is seated on the throne, who lives for ever and ever" (Revelation 4:9).

When we have a special request to ask of God, do we accompany it by thanking God in advance for what is to come? Our focus is not on outcomes but on what the Most High decrees for our good. In other words, we give thanks *before* we receive whatever gifts God bestows. In this way we avoid the temptation to replace thankfulness by somber expressions of disappointment. We ready our hearts to see the lavish love of God that offsets human cruelty. We thank God for past revelations of divine protection as well as for graces yet to be revealed.

Countless other examples could be given to prove that, without exercising the virtue of thanksgiving, it would be difficult, if not impossible, to resist the pull of a depreciative, self-indulgent society. The portal to appreciation is this ability to believe in God's care renewed daily on our behalf. Rather than approaching adversity by becoming anxious or obsessive, rather than letting animosity overload us with anger and frustration, we thank God that for us a mountain of insurmountable difficulty has been shrunk to a mustard seed of unshakeable faith, undying hope, and unmitigated love.

LET US PRAY

Lord, protect me from being beguiled by selfish claims that bypass the always-ample evidence of Your bestowal of grace. Make me mindful of the commission to be a good steward over earth and water, sea and sky. Let me remember that my life remains an unfinished story with chapters full of gratitude that are yet to be written. Let the virtue of thanksgiving widen my vision of Your omnipresence. Help me to respond with due appreciation to the bounty I behold in my everyday world. Grant me a glimpse of the part I play in the symphony of eternal thanks pervading cosmos and humanity and calling every molecule of life into being.

CHAPTER 28

SERENITY

I therefore, a prisoner for the Lord, beg you to lead a life worthy of
the calling to which you have been called, with all lowliness and meekness,
with patience, forbearing one another in love. (Ephesians 4:1–2)

From nearby neighborhoods to distant lands, violence threatens to crush the goal of peace people of good will seek. However many diplomatic efforts we make, however numerous the reconciliation conferences we hold, the harmony that would bring a bit of heaven to earth eludes us. Worldly attempts, political and social, to find lasting serenity are worth pursuing but the stated goal may not be reached. Perhaps the Prince of Peace knew how difficult the task before us would be. After all, His farewell gift to us was His peace—a gift whose fullness the world cannot fathom. Genocidal blows continue to crush each person's dignity. Chaos threatens serenity in many parts of our planet. Such failures must prompt renewed calls for prayer. To follow Christ is to find peace within and to accept the commission to be a peacemaker, but how does this happen?

One way is to resolve minor disagreements before they escalate into a worsening disposition of animosity. Our efforts to make peace may be beset by friend and foe alike, but no obstacle ought to paralyze our hope that one day Jesus' farewell gift of peace will prevail (cf. John 14:27). Raging storms will grow calm. Relationships will improve. Irritation will give way to relaxation, conflict to contentment.

To prepare to be messengers of peace wherever God places us, we need to cultivate a more tranquil way of being—one less bombarded by media-fueled distractions day and night. Work without rest pulls us apart like plucked chickens. We run in different directions at once. The more decentered we become, the less likely we are to keep company with the Prince of Peace dwelling in the inmost center of our being.

What the Lord expects of us is neither to make peace at any price nor to give up this cause in despair of its success. We must continue to uphold the Gospel vision that names as the fruits of the Spirit love, joy, and peace (cf. Galatians 5:22).

Peacemaking in Christ's name inspires us to start to mitigate controversy around the family dinner table, to say nothing of trying to prevent the escalation of one country's domination of another. In a universe scarred by warring factions, this beatitude is not a luxury but a necessity. We may be given a taste of what Christ intended when we put a stop to familial bickering; when we set aside agendas that only cause more controversy, and when we seek mutual forgiveness after the rules of humane engagement have been nearly hacked into oblivion.

Any evidence of a return to equanimity gives us cause to rejoice. From this calmer place of grace, we can wait upon the Lord with open hands, ready to respond serenely should He call on us to be His ambassadors. If and when others fail to understand our best intentions, we avoid discouragement by setting sail toward the peaceful harbor Christ provides until the stormy clouds pass. Only if we overcome the barriers to harmony in our own heart can we be carriers of God's harmonious presence to others.

LET US PRAY

Lord, quell the dictates of stubborn willfulness that disrupt both my inner life and my outer world. When circumstances beyond my control shatter my hopes for serenity, give me the courage to attune them to the pace of Your grace. More than the cessation of conflict, such tranquility gives me pause to consider other ways to be a peacemaker. May the seeds of Your prayer for peace be planted in my soul and bear good fruit in the midst of persecution by the Evil One. Let my efforts in this regard, however minor they may be, begin to heal the human race and gather us, one and all, under the shadow of Your wings (Psalm 17:8).

AFTERWORD

There are times when the lens through which we look for clues to virtuous living seems to let little or no light through. Often we bound out of bed in the morning, ready to make the best of the day, only to be greeted by an onslaught of media-fueled bad news. Just when we feel we have turned a corner from infidelity to fidelity or from anger to forgiveness or from doubt to trust or from greed to generosity, we find ourselves overwhelmed by certain inner and outer forces over which we seem to have no control.

Despite the many means of grace granted to us to be countercultural Christians, we may weaken in our resolve when we are told that "if it feels good, it is good," a slogan arising from moral relativism that tries to convince us that as long as we do our own thing, nothing else matters. Such narcissistic attitudes lead to indifference to one's neighbor, to the despisal of authority in any form, and to a devaluation of commitment.

A quick fix that does not solve this crisis of virtuous living is a reliance on exterior plans, programs, and projects to ward off the terror of a world seemingly abandoned by God. In a religionless age, treating persons in dehumanizing ways begins to seem acceptable. We fail to see that unless we change our hearts, we cannot transform the world.

The answer may lie less in verbal debates and defenses and more in a silent but supreme confidence in the Word made flesh who dwells among us. When we are at our weakest, Christ manifests Himself as our strength. When we wonder if assistance is at hand, we may simply reply, "Our help is in the name of the Lord, who has made heaven and earth" (Psalm 124:8).

The virtuous life rejects the autonomous claim that we can save ourselves. It signifies unshakeable confidence in the promise of God that happiness lies not in narcissistic inventions leading to instant gratification but in nurturing our passion for the impossible under the sovereignty of our Savior. Faith in His Word reveals the falsehood embedded in pessimistic acceptance of a predetermined fate. We grow in wisdom, age, and grace not on the basis of our own cleverness but due to a profound, inner change of heart.

As I have tried to show in this book, we must be willing, among other goals, to proclaim the truth that even when we abandon God, God never deserts us. Waiting upon the Lord with patience and perseverance implies watching. While we may not know the day or the hour set for the coming of the Lord, nothing can shake our confidence that He will shatter our deafness and speak to our souls a directive worth pursuing.

To pray from the heart is to offer the Lord free reign over our lives. A sense of meaning never leaves us when ordinary days become pointers to the transcendent. God's promise is being fulfilled in ways we can neither predict nor imagine nor fully understand. Virtuous living means to celebrate everydayness as an epiphany of the mystery and to behold in the richness of the ordinary ways that prove God is always with us.

Now is the time to let go of utopian schemes of self-salvation and accept the limits of life as reminders of our need for redemption. We hear the voice of virtue spoken in our heart and in the words of the spiritual masters, who guide our journey of formation. We pray that our reply to the question of life's meaning will echo St. Teresa of Avila's inspiring bookmark prayer:

> Let nothing disturb you,
> Nothing affright you.
> All things are passing;
> God never changes.
> Patient endurance
> Attains to all things.
> Whoever possesses God
> Is wanting in nothing.
> God alone suffices.[1]

This formula for virtuous living can be relied upon to counter any vice detailed in the appendix to this book. I invite everyone who reads it to remember that "the unexamined life is not worth living."[2] Where vice once held us in chains in the shadowy corners of sin, the light of virtue continues to shine and evil has met its match.

---

1 The "bookmark" of St. Theresa of -Avila, written in her Breviary.
2 Socrates, Plato's *Apology*, 38a.

APPENDIX

BEYOND SIN TO SALVATION:
LOOSENING THE GRIP OF VICE ON OUR SOUL

Virtuous living—consisting of our efforts to foster what is good and resist what is evil—is under continual attack by vices that threaten to bring ruin to our edifice of virtue unless we maintain strict vigilance. We must not live in the naïve assumption that these capital sins are so heinous that we need not worry about falling into bondage because of them. They are part and parcel of our fallen condition. Avoiding entrapment in them is the work of a lifetime. Only with the help of grace may we be able to grow beyond pride to humility, beyond greed to generosity, beyond anger to patience, beyond dejection to delight, beyond sloth to service, beyond gluttony to moderation, and beyond lustful living to chaste loving.

Many masters of the spiritual life come to our aid in this struggle, three of whose teachings are especially efficacious. One is the first codifier of the "eight vices," Evagrius Ponticus (345–399)[1]; the other is his disciple, St. John Cassian (360–435), who analyzes the evil

---

[1] Evagrius Ponticus, *The Praktikos*, Chapters *On Prayer*, trans. John Eudes Bamberger, OCSO (Spencer, MA: Cistercian Publications, 1970).

thoughts that lead to the actions that strip virtue from the soul.[2] The third is a medieval master and doctor of the Church, St. John of the Cross (1542–1591). In his masterpiece, *The Dark Night*,[3] he discusses from a spiritual perspective the dispositions to the seven deadly sins, defined in the sixth century by St. Gregory the Great. He shows, for example, that "spiritual gluttony" may lead to the hoarding of feelings, causing one to question his or her fidelity to Christ when aridity or felt desolation prevails over once prevalent consolations.

These masters show us in no uncertain terms that vice is the archenemy of virtue. They turn to Scripture and Tradition for descriptions of the virtuous life and its rewards. They encourage us to pursue the goal of beatitude to which grace and our cooperation with it may lead us. The masters convince us of the degree to which these capital sins damage and obscure our potential for conformity to Christ without destroying it entirely.

BEYOND PRIDE TO HUMILITY

St. John Cassian calls the demon of pride sinister, especially because nothing makes the devil salivate more than his seeking "to destroy those who have mounted almost to the heights of holiness."[4] Cassian continues: "Just as a deadly plague destroys not just one member of the body, but the whole of it, so pride corrupts the whole soul, not just part of it. Each of the other passions that trouble the soul attacks and tries to overcome the single virtue which is opposed to it, and so it darkens and troubles the soul only partially. But the passion of pride darkens the soul completely and leads to its utter downfall."[5]

The analysis the master offers as to why pride is so deadly enables him to introduce several other capital sins as killers of body, mind, and

---

2 St. John Cassian, "On the Eight Vices" in *The Philokalia*, compiled by St. Nikodimos of the Holy Mountain and St. Makarios of Corinth, Vol. 1, trans. G. E. H. Palmer, Philip Sherrard, Kallistos Ware (London: Faber and Faber, 1979).

3 St. John of the Cross, *The Dark Night*, in *The Collected Works*, trans. Kieran Kavanaugh, OCD and Otilio Rodriguez, OCD (Washington, DC: Institute of Carmelite Studies, 1991).

4 Cassian, *Philokalia*, 92.

5 Ibid., 92.

spirit. Gluttony tries to destroy self-control; unchastity, moderation; avarice, voluntary poverty; anger, gentleness; and so on with the other vices. When pride has become the master of our soul, it acts like a harsh tyrant who has gained control of a great city, destroying it completely and razing it to ruin. Cassian attributes to this demon a detrimental envy of God and of God's preferred creatures: you and me. The angel of light, Lucifer, became the prince of darkness who thought of himself as the equal of God. Like the serpent that slithered into the psyche of Adam and Eve, so Satan roams around seeking whom he may devour:

> Since we are aware of this, we should feel fear and guard our hearts with extreme care from the deadly spirit of pride. When we have attained some degree of holiness we should always repeat to ourselves the words of the Apostle: "Yet not I, but the grace of God which was with me" (1 Corinthians 15:10), as well as what was said by the Lord: "Without me you can do nothing" (John 15:5).[6]

It goes without saying that the only virtue powerful enough to combat this enemy is humility. With the Apostle Paul we ought to ask, "What have you that you did not receive? If then you received it, why do you boast as if it were not a gift?" (1 Corinthians 4:7). What gives us the bloated boastfulness to think that we could achieve perfection through our own efforts? Salvation is ours through the grace and mercy of God. As Cassian concludes, "All of our holy fathers knew this and all with one accord teach that perfection in holiness can be achieved only through humility. Humility, in its turn, can be achieved only through faith, fear of God, gentleness and the shedding of all possessions. It is by means of these that we attain perfect love, through the grace and compassion of our Lord Jesus Christ, to whom be glory through the ages."[7]

---

6 Ibid., 93.
7 Ibid., 93.

Many years separate Cassian from John of the Cross, but their thoughts coalesce when pride enters the picture. It is John's purpose in Book One of *The Dark Night* to discuss the damage to the spirit caused by the seven capital sins. He observes that spiritual pride breeds complacency and a lack of dependence on God in all that we are and do. We become proud of our accomplishments and forget to give credit to God in a spirit of self-effacing humility.

Spiritual pride causes us to become overly attached to the projects of self-salvation we devise. It tempts us to adopt an "I can do it alone" or "we can do it alone" mentality. The "demon of narcissism" blocks our reliance on grace and hinders the desire to give our life to the service of God and neighbor. As St. John observes,

> Many want to be the favorites of their confessors, and thus they are consumed by a thousand envies and disquietudes. Embarrassment forbids them from relating their sins clearly, lest their reputation diminish in their confessor's eye. They confess their sins in a most favorable light so as to appear better than they actually are, and thus they approach the confessional to excuse themselves rather than accuse themselves. Sometimes they confess the evil things they do to a different confessor so that their own confessor might think they commit no sins at all. Therefore, in their desire to appear holy, they enjoy relating their good behavior to their confessor, and in such careful terms that these good deeds appear greater than they actually are. It would be more humble of them . . . to make light of the good they do and to wish that no one, neither their confessor nor anybody else, should consider it of any importance at all.[8]

Docility, the desire to be directed by God, and not by any prideful claim to self-sufficiency, facilitates the purging of spiritual pride and opens the floodgates of the heart to the healing power of humility.

8 John of the Cross, *The Dark Night*, 2:4, 363–364.

St. John describes what happens to souls advancing by the grace of God to spiritual perfection on this well-trod path.

> [They] act in an entirely different manner and with a different quality of spirit. They receive great benefit from their humility, by which they not only place little importance on their deeds, but also take very little self-satisfaction from them. They think everyone else is far better than they are, and usually possess a holy envy of them and would like to emulate their service of God. Since they are truly humble, their growing fervor and the increased number of their good deeds and the gratification they receive from them only cause them to become more aware of their debt to God and the inadequacy of their service to him, and thus the more they do, the less satisfaction they derive from it. Their charity and love make them want to do so much for God that what they actually do accomplish seems as nothing. This loving solicitude goads them, preoccupies them, and absorbs them to such an extent that they never notice what others do or do not accomplish, but if they should, they then think, as I say, that everyone is better than they. They think they themselves are insignificant, and want others to think this also and to belittle and slight their deeds. Moreover, even though others do praise and value their works, these souls are unable to believe them; such praises seem strange to them.[9]

Returning to the desert tradition, notably to *The Praktikos* of Evagrius Ponticus, we are told that the spirit of vainglory or self-esteem is a subtle expansion of the "demon of pride" and its deadly consequences. It is what leads one to hunt after praise and to put one's struggle for holiness before the Holy whom one desires. Vainglory is the breeding ground of pride, which cajoles one into denying that God is one's helper and the cause of all of one's virtuous actions. In the words of Evagrius "[one] gets a big head in regard to the brethren,

---

9 Ibid., 2:6, 364.

considering them stupid because they do not all have this same opinion of him."[10]

All of these masters agree that the best way to cultivate humility is to do more spiritual reading, to pray unceasingly, and to remember to live in the presence of the divine Presence at all times. Such contemplative remembrance helps to block the thoughts that lead to vainglory and the vices that surround it like anger and resentment. According to Evagrius, "When a man has once attained to contemplative knowledge and the delight that derives from it he will no longer yield himself up to the demon of vainglory, though the demon offer all the delights of the world to him. For what, may I ask, could surpass spiritual contemplation?"[11]

As an aid to humility, Evagrius reminds us to ponder our former life and our past sins and to thank God that we were brought to peace and tranquility (*apatheia*) only by the redemptive love and forgiveness of Jesus Christ. Grace alone has enabled us to separate ourselves from worldliness, that brought us to such low points of vainglory and pride, and to remember that we are mere creatures, not the Creator. As he assures us, "such thoughts instill humility in us and afford no entrance to the demon of pride."[12]

BEYOND GREED TO GENEROSITY

Whereas pride corrodes our heart from within, it is Cassian's contention that the demon of avarice attacks us from without, mainly because we lack trust in God's providence and hedge our bets with the fullest of barns. If we think for one minute that this demon will drift off, we are sorely mistaken. Avarice is like an exotic taste that makes us crave for more; it convinces us that enough is never enough. Neglect to temper greed and it will, in Cassian's words, "become harder to get rid of and more destructive than the other passions, for according to the Apostle it is 'the root of all evil' (1 Timothy 6:10)."[13]

---

10 Evagrius Ponticus, *The Praktikos*, 14:20.
11 Ibid., 32:24.
12 Ibid., 33:25.
13 Cassian, *Philokalia*, 78.

Avarice represents a perversion of our free will. Instead of choosing to be generous, we become collectors and hoarders of material goods. With full coffers, one imagines no harm will come to one. Avarice "conjures up in a monk's mind a picture of a lengthy old age and bodily illness; and it persuades him that the necessities of life provided by the monastery are insufficient to sustain a healthy man, much less an ill one; that in the monastery the sick, instead of receiving proper attention, are hardly cared for at all; and that unless he has some money tucked away, he will die a miserable death. Finally, it convinces him that he will not be able to remain long in the monastery because of the load of his work and the strictness of the abbot."[14]

The result is easy to see: the monk forfeits his vow of poverty, for the right reasons, of course, and gives himself, "completely . . . over to the thought of gain." Money becomes his god—an all too familiar scenario in our world today. The greedy person

> fixes his intellect on the love, not of God, but of the images of men stamped on gold. A monk darkened by such thoughts and launched on the downward path can no longer be obedient. He is irritable and resentful, and grumbles about every task. He answers back and, having lost his sense of respect, behaves like a stubborn, uncontrollable horse. He is not satisfied with the day's ration of food and complains that he cannot put up with such conditions for ever. Neither God's presence, he says, nor the possibility of his own salvation is confined to the monastery; and, he concludes, he will perish if he does not leave it. He is so excited and encouraged in these perverse thoughts by his secret hoardings that he even plans to quit the monastery. Then he replies proudly and harshly no matter what he is told to do, and pays no heed if he sees something in the monastery that needs to be set right, considering himself a stranger and outsider and finding fault with all that takes place. Then he seeks excuses for being angry or injured, so that he

---

14 Ibid., 78–79.

will not appear to be leaving the monastery frivolously and without cause. He does not even shrink from trying through gossip and idle talk to seduce someone else into leaving with him, wishing to have an accomplice in his sinful action."[15]

The picture Cassian paints of a monk gone bad could be repeated from Wall Street to almost any street in town. Avarice is a terrible sin since it not only hurts the hoarder but harms many other innocent people. Witness the fate of a Bernie Madoff, imprisoned for one hundred and fifty years for crimes of greed that ruined hundreds of investors who trusted him.

According to St. John of the Cross, *spiritual avarice* leads to possessiveness of heart and to keeping our eyes fixed on non-tangible possessions (images and ideas) rather than on the divine Owner to whom belongs all that we possess of inner and outer goods.

Spiritual avarice, like its material counterpart, breeds endless discontent in the soul. One always wants more of what will never satisfy one anyway. That is why such greedy souls

> become unhappy and peevish because they don't find the consolation they want in spiritual things. Many never have enough of hearing counsels, or learning spiritual maxims, or keeping them and reading books about them. They spend more time in these than in striving after mortification and the perfection of the interior poverty to which they are obliged.
>
> Furthermore, they weight themselves down with over decorated images and rosaries. They now put these down, now take up others; at one moment they are exchanging, and at the next re-exchanging. Now they want this kind, now they want another. And they prefer one cross to another because of its elaborateness. Others you see who are decked out in *agnusdeis* and relics and lists of saints' names, like children in trinkets.[16]

---

15 Ibid., 79.
16 John of the Cross, *The Dark Night*, 3:1, 365–366.

Inordinate attachments like these despoil the possibility of living in poverty of spirit. One becomes possessed by one's possessions and cannot be free until avarice is uprooted from one's heart. Generosity of spirit—loving self and neighbor in God and for God's sake—facilitates the purging of spiritual avarice, but to acquire this virtue calls for great interior detachment based on pleasing God and not ourselves. As St. John observes,

> I knew a person who for more than ten years profited by a cross roughly made out of a blessed palm and held together by a pin twisted around it. That person carried it about and never would part with it until I took it—and the person was not someone of poor judgment or little intelligence. I saw someone else who prayed with beads made out of bones from the spine of a fish. Certainly, the devotion was not for this reason less precious in the sight of God. In neither of these two instances, obviously, did these persons base their own devotion on the workmanship and value of a spiritual object.
>
> They, therefore, who are well guided from the outside do not become attached to visible instruments or burden themselves with them. They do not care to know any more than is necessary to accomplish good works, because their eyes are fixed only on God, on being his friend and pleasing him; this is what they long for. They very generously give all they have. Their pleasure is to know how to live for love of God or neighbor without these spiritual or temporal things. As I say, they set their eyes on the substance of interior perfection, on pleasing God and not themselves.[17]

In the desert tradition, as represented in *The Praktikos* of Evagrius Ponticus, as well as in the description of the vices in Cassian's account, when greed grips the soul, it is impossible for charity (generosity) to exist in it (cf. Matthew 26:14). It was the greed already implanted in

---

17 Ibid., 3:2, 366.

Judas' heart that blocked Jesus' appeal to self-giving love. Whereas the generous heart seeks to part with money and, in a spirit of almsgiving, to foster the wise use of possessions and never to be possessed by them, the greedy heart closes off the floodgates of self-giving.

Avarice flings many obstacles on the path to holiness including the inability to perform manual labor, the forgetfulness of famines and sicknesses that are bound to come, and the shame one will feel when "the bubble breaks" of having to accept help from others to meet life's necessities.[18] Neither must we forget that one evil thought leads to another. For example, if one loves money as one's "god" and fails to amass enough of it, one will become angry and dejected.

To counteract the demon of greed, it might be wise to meditate on the following passages from Holy Scripture.

In Colossians 3:5, St. Paul confirms the connection between greed and idolatry and says that we must be on guard if we are to cast off idols and clothe ourselves with a new self whose chief character trait is generosity. As the Apostle James reminds us: "Every good endowment and every perfect gift is from above, coming down from the Father of lights with whom there is no variation or shadow due to change" (James 1:17). Also, the Apostle Paul says that the fruits of the Spirit by which we must be known are "love, joy, peace, patience, kindness, goodness, faithfulness, gentleness, [and] self-control" (Galatians 5:22–23).

BEYOND ANGER TO PATIENCE

All of us have had the experience of being caught in a burst of almost uncontrollable anger. From temper-tantrums to road rage, none of us has a firewall to protect us from this vengeful demon, which Cassian calls "a deadly poison" that, with God's help, we must eradicate from the depths of our souls. He adds: "So long as he dwells in our hearts and blinds the eyes of the heart with his somber disorders, we can neither discriminate what is for our good, nor achieve spiritual knowledge, nor fulfill our good intentions, nor participate in true life;

---

18 Evagrius Ponticus, *The Praktikos*, 9:17.

and our intellect will remain impervious to the contemplation of the true divine light; for it is written, 'My eyes waste away because of grief; they grow weak because of all my woes' (Psalm 6:7)."[19]

Anger is food for fools, but wiser people are not immune from its force. Just let an irritating person or an unexpectedly demeaning episode come our way, and the searing flame of anger may destroy common sense; dispel vigilance of heart; hurt others, and cause us to lose, in Cassian's words, our "decorum and dignity." Speaking directly to us, he says:

> If, therefore, you desire to attain perfection and rightly to pursue the spiritual way, you should make yourself a stranger to all sinful anger and wrath. Listen to what St. Paul enjoins: "Rid yourselves of all bitterness, wrath, anger, clamor, evil speaking and all malice" (Ephesians 4:31). In saying "all" he leaves no excuse for regarding any anger as necessary or reasonable. If you want to correct your brother when he is doing wrong or to punish him, you must try to keep yourself calm; otherwise you yourself may catch the sickness you now apply to him: "Physician, heal yourself" (Luke 4:23), or "Why do you look at the speck of dust in your brother's eye, and not notice the rafter in your own eye?" (Matthew 7:3).[20]

The bevy of deformative dispositions that trail in anger's wake ought to remind us of how dangerous it is. Even in its righteous form, as when Jesus threw the moneychangers out of the temple, it has to be followed by forgiveness. Anger is dangerous because it obstructs our spiritual vision. This incensive power has to be monitored with care lest it lead to impassioned, self-indulgent thoughts:

> This is what the Prophet teaches us when he says: "Be angry, and do not sin" (Psalm 4:4)—that is, be angry with your own passions and with your malicious thoughts,

---

19 *Cassian, Philokalia*, 82.
20 Ibid., 83.

and do not sin by carrying out their suggestions. . . .
That is, when malicious thoughts enter your heart,
expel them with anger, and then turn to compunction
and repentance as if your soul were resting in a bed
of stillness."[21]

No wonder the Lord commands us to leave our offering at the
altar and be reconciled with our brother (cf. Matthew 5:23–24).
Otherwise, our offering will not be acceptable. So long as anger and
fury are bottled up within us, how can we hope to imitate Christ?
Prayer is the best antidote for this poison. We know from experience
that rancor cancels the plea for reconciliation and that quarreling
disquiets our soul. Self-reform is a long process since:

> Unhealed passions . . . are merely hidden, not erased;
> for unless our passions are first purged, solitude and
> withdrawal from the world not only foster them but
> also keep them concealed, no longer allowing us to
> perceive what passion it is that enslaves us. On the
> contrary, they impose on us an illusion of virtue and
> persuade us to believe that we have achieved long-
> suffering and humility, because there is no one present
> to provoke and test us. But as soon as something
> happens which does arouse and challenge us, our
> hidden and previously unnoticed passions immediately
> break out like uncontrolled horses that have long been
> kept unexercised and idle, dragging their driver all the
> more violently and wildly to destruction.[22]

Cassian's insights into the human psyche are universal and
timeless. The resolution of anger does not happen by hiding from
other people. Rage only grows worse and the patience we thought we
possessed in isolation is an illusion. Cassian uses the following analogy
to prove his point:

---

21 Ibid., 83.
22 Ibid., 85.

Poisonous creatures that live quietly in their lairs in the desert display their fury only when they detect someone approaching; and likewise passion-filled men, who live quietly not because of their virtuous disposition but because of their solitude, spit forth their venom whenever someone approaches and provokes them. This is why those seeking perfect gentleness must make every effort to avoid anger not only towards men, but also towards animals and even inanimate objects.[23]

However angry we become we must not smash the piano or kick the cat! Cassian admits to such a temptation:

I can remember how, when I lived in the desert, I became angry with the rushes because they were either too thick or too thin; or with a piece of wood, when I wished to cut it quickly and could not; or with a flint, when I was in a hurry to light a fire and the spark would not come. So all-embracing was my anger that it was aroused even against inanimate objects."[24]

Is there any lasting cure for this sickness? Only one suffices and that is not becoming furious for any reason whatsoever, whether just or unjust, unless we are prepared to forgive both ourselves and others. Because this demon darkens our mind we lose the light of discernment; good judgment may abandon us momentarily. Our soul ceases to be a temple of the Holy Spirit when we lose self-restraint. Cassian reminds us that the renunciation of material things, to say nothing of fasting and vigils, are not of any benefit if at the last judgment we are found to have been the slaves of anger and hatred.

St. John of the Cross associates spiritual anger with the petty response of "peevishness." When any irritating person, event, or situation over which we have no control crosses our path, we feel a sudden cramp in our psyche. Accompanying this state of sullenness

23 Ibid., 85.
24 Ibid., 85–86.

may be an indiscreet zeal for pushing our own ideas or plans on others. So impatient are we to make quick progress in the spiritual life that we get angry at ourselves, others, and God when we fail to "become saints in a day!"

This "crevice in our heart" into which the demonic slips weakens the dispositions of waiting upon God and conforming to holier invitations, challenges, and appeals. Instead, anger and the pushy impatience it breeds lead to broken resolutions and foster the "blame game."

Angry people become peevish in the works they do and easily angered at the least obstacle they encounter. According to St. John, whose experience in community no one can doubt, they may be occasionally so unbearable that nobody can put up with them. No sooner do they experience some pleasant sensation in prayer than they feel "vapid and zestless" if it does not repeat itself. They act like children "withdrawn from the sweet breast" and at the least provocation they may erupt in a tempter-tantrum. The saint adds that such an imperfection can only be purged "through the dryness and distress of the dark night."[25]

What other altercations does spiritual anger foster? Among those already mentioned by St. John, two more stand out. Due to indiscreet zeal, one becomes angry over the sins of others, reproves them harshly, and sets oneself up as a paragon of virtue, conduct contrary to spiritual meekness. In becoming aware of their own imperfections, others grow angry with themselves in a spirit of unhumble impatience. They make numerous plans and resolutions, but since they are not humble and have no distrust of themselves, the more resolves they make the more they break, and the greater becomes their anger. They do not have patience to wait until God gives them what they need, when He so desires. Their attitude, which is contrary to docility, can only be remedied by the sheer grace of God. So angered are they about their desire for advancement, it might be wiser to conclude that God would prefer them to be a little less demonstrative.

---

25 John of the Cross, *The Dark Night*, 5:1, 370.

In the desert tradition, that compliments these astute observations, Evagrius Ponticus identifies anger as "the most fierce passion." He defines it as a "boiling and stirring up of wrath against one who has given injury—or is thought to have done so."[26]

One way to befuddle this demon is to "nip" the irritation we feel towards others in the bud before it seeps further into our soul. This demon's favored mode of operation is, according to Evagrius, to attack us at the time of prayer. All the old hurts we continue to harbor have a tendency to rush into our mind. In a flash we see the "picture of the offensive person before our eyes." If we allow this feeling to persist, it will be transformed into indignation and lack of forgiveness. Evagrius confirms the scriptural counsel not to let the sun go down on our anger "lest by night the demons come upon us to strike fear in our souls and render our spirits more cowardly for the fight on the morrow."[27]

The masters agree that we must not give ourselves over to angry thoughts but replace them quickly with compassion and forgiveness. We leave ultimate judgment in God's hands while making whatever practical judgments are necessary to honor the demands of justice, peace, and mercy. By so doing, we cultivate the virtue of patience, remembering that God Himself is "merciful and gracious, slow to anger, and abounding in steadfast love and faithfulness" (Exodus 34:6) and that God's anger "is but for a moment" (Psalm 30:5).

BEYOND DEJECTION TO DELIGHT

One mark of Cassian's genius is that he numbers among the capital sins that of dejection. He compares it to an arrow that punctures the heart by virtue of the hatred shown to people of prayer by the so-called noonday devil. This "demon of dejection" obscures the soul's capacity for spiritual contemplation and keeps it from doing good works. So malicious is this attack that the demon seizes our soul and darkens it

---

26 Evagrius Ponticus, *The Praktikos*, 11:18.
27 Ibid., 21:21.

completely, "[preventing] us from praying gladly, from reading Holy Scripture with profit and perseverance, and from being gentle and compassionate towards our brethren."[28] The tactics employed by this clever devil include instilling "a hatred of every kind of work and even of the monastic profession itself. Undermining all the soul's salutary resolutions, weakening its persistence and constancy, he leaves it senseless and paralyzed, tied and bound by its despairing thoughts."[29]

In today's parlance we might speak of low-grade depression or of ministry burnout. Unfortunately, in a climate of psychological sophistication, we might be inclined to overlook or even laugh at the thought of a "demon of dejection," but Cassian is convinced of its presence and counsels us to guard our heart:

> Just as a moth devours clothing and a worm devours wood, so dejection devours a man's soul. It persuades him to shun every helpful encounter and stops him from accepting advice from his true friends or giving them a courteous and peaceful reply. Seizing the entire soul, it fills it with bitterness and listlessness. Then it suggests to souls that they should go away from other people, since they are the cause of their agitation. It does not allow the soul to understand that its sickness does not come from without, but lies hidden within, only manifesting itself when temptations attack the soul because of its ascetic efforts. [30]

Just as a fever flares up and subsides, only to rise again at the least provocation, so a sickness like this can at any moment recur and cause us to lose hope. The demon seems to demand success and to make us feel like failures when we do not achieve it. Blessed Charles de Foucauld counters this hangdog tendency by telling us: "Let us thank God a thousand times if in the sadness which invades us it seems to us as if we are rejected by the world. The depression and suffering, the

---

28 Cassian, *Philokalia*, 87.
29 Ibid., 87.
30 Ibid., 87.

bitterness with which we seem sometimes to be soaked, were the lot of our Lord on earth."[31]

If we are to defeat the demon that casts our soul into despair, we need to examine what it is that triggers dejection. Among other causes, it could be failed relationships and unmet expectations; a mismatch between our idle dreams and what God wills; a climate of depreciation in the work force; or an overriding suspicion of anyone in authority—what right do they have to tell us what to do? Cassian is even more strict about why we must drive this demon from our heart:

> It was this demon that did not allow Cain to repent after he had killed his brother, or Judas after he had betrayed his Master. The only form of dejection we should cultivate is the sorrow which goes with repentance for sin and is accompanied by hope in God. It was of this form of dejection that the Apostle said: "Godly sorrow produces a saving repentance which is not to be repented of" (2 Corinthians 7:10). This "godly sorrow" nourishes the soul through the hope engendered by repentance, and it is mingled with joy. That is why it makes us obedient and eager for every good work: accessible, humble, gentle, forbearing and patient in enduring all the suffering or tribulation God may send us.[32]

The "godly sorrow" that reverses self-pity and dejection allows us to enjoy the fruits of the Holy Spirit: love, joy, peace, long-suffering, goodness, faith, self-control (cf. Galatians 5:22). By contrast, to the degree that dejection prevails, we risk imbibing the fruits of the evil spirit: listlessness, impatience, anger, hatred, contentiousness, despair, and sluggishness in praying. Cassian concludes: "We should shun this second form of dejection as we would unchastity, avarice, anger and the rest of the passions. It can be healed by prayer, hope in God, meditation on Holy Scripture, and by living with godly people."[33] The

---

31 Charles De Foucauld, *Meditations of a Hermit*, Second Revised edition (London: Burns & Oates, 1981), 135.
32 Cassian, *Philokalia*, 88.
33 Ibid., 88.

latter help us to focus on God's capacity to save us, instead of on our own incapacity to do anything right. Such witnesses to hope pass on all that bolsters us in our faith tradition, starting with the knowledge of God's love for us. They are the first to point out our giftedness and to encourage us to stay on the path set by faith—not in any expectation of worldly success but in the desire to remain committed to our calling in Christ.

Dejection in John Cassian's analysis is analogous to what St. John of the Cross identifies as *melancholia* (or melancholy). According to the saint, it is a deficiency of sense or spirit that ought not to be identified as such with the "dark night." Nonetheless, it is a serious obstacle to wholesome and harmonious spiritual growth. By the same token, spiritual aridity, with the trials and conflicts it evokes, must not be dismissed by saying that such dryness in prayer is due to melancholia, a depressed temperament, or a feeling that perhaps, because of an unrecognized wickedness, God has forsaken us. Similarly, the disinclination to make discursive meditations, for example, on a text from Holy Scripture, may not be due to God's calling us to a quiet style of prayer but only to "melancholia" that affects our ability to think or act at all. St. John reminds us of the role the demonic plays in disquieting and disturbing our souls when he relates "spiritual lust" to "melancholia." It is the devil's work

> to bring disquietude and disturbance on a soul when it is praying, or trying to pray, [then] he endeavors to excite impure feelings in the sensory part. And if people pay any attention to these, the devil does them great harm. Through fear, some souls grow slack in their prayer—which is what the devil wants—in order to struggle against these movements, and others give it up entirely, for they think these feelings come while they are engaged in prayer rather than at other times. And this is true because the devil excites these feelings while souls are at prayer, instead of when they are engaged in other works, so that they might abandon prayer. And

that is not all; to make them cowardly and afraid, he brings vividly to their minds foul and impure thoughts. And sometimes the thoughts will concern spiritually helpful things and persons. Those who attribute any importance to such thoughts, therefore, do not even dare look at anything or think about anything lest they thereupon stumble into them.[34]

Whereas some of us may be inclined to mock people who suffer from this malady, St. John displays the opposite inclination.

These impure thoughts so affect people who are afflicted with melancholia that one should have great pity for them; indeed, these people suffer a sad life. In some who are troubled with this bad humor the trial reaches such a point that they clearly feel that the devil has access to them without their having the freedom to prevent it. Yet some of these melancholics are able through intense effort and struggle to forestall this power of the devil. If these impure thoughts and feelings arise from melancholia, individuals are not ordinarily freed from them until they are cured of that humor—unless they enter the dark night, which in time deprives them of everything.[35]

Wise spiritual director that he is, St. John advises us to distinguish spiritual dryness (aridity) from luke-warmness (dejection due to one's being "lax and remiss in their will and spirit, and [having] no solicitude about serving God"[36]). One experiencing genuine "purgative dryness" is "ordinarily solicitous, concerned, and pained about not serving God," says St. John,

even though the dryness may be furthered by melancholia or some other humor—as it often is—it does not thereby fail to produce its purgative effect

---

34 John of the Cross, *The Dark Night*, 4:3, 368.
35 Ibid., 4:3, 368.
36 Ibid., 9:3, 378.

in the appetite, for the soul will be deprived of every satisfaction and concerned only about God. If this humor is the entire cause, everything ends in displeasure and does harm to one's nature, and there are none of these desires to serve God that accompany the purgative dryness. Even though in this purgative dryness the sensory part of the soul is very cast down, slack, and feeble in its actions because of the little satisfaction it finds, the spirit is ready and strong.[37]

It is at this point in our quest for Christian maturity that St. John helps us to shift from dejection to delight. Two of the benefits of the purgative way are the grace of habitual remembrance of God and the bestowal upon us of a peace and joy that surpasses understanding. He says that unexpected touches, delights, and favors from God may occur suddenly, often in the midst of aridity. Due to the harmonizing of our sensate life with the operations of the transcendent, we are less likely to suffer from the dissonant effects of dejection, depletion of energy, and depression.

Evagrius Ponticus confirms both Cassian's and St. John's concern regarding what he names "sadness."[38] It can occur for a number of reasons, including not getting our own way or plunging into dejection because the fantasy in which we have indulged cannot be realized. In a split second, the noonday devil may slip into the crevice in our heart that we have created. What happens then is not only an escalation of dejection but of any number of other vices.

[The demon] presses his attack upon the monk about the fourth hour and besieges the soul until the eighth hour. First of all, he makes it seem that the sun barely moves, if at all, and that the day is fifty hours long. Then he constrains the monk to look constantly out the windows, to walk outside the cell, to gaze carefully at the sun to determine how far it stands from the ninth hour, to look now this way and now that to see

---

37 Ibid., 9:3, 378.
38 Evagrius Ponticus, *The Praktikos*, 10:17–18.

if perhaps [one of the brethren appears from his cell]. Then too he instills in the heart of the monk a hatred for the place, a hatred for his very life itself, a hatred for manual labor. He leads him to reflect that charity has departed from among the brethren, that there is no one to give encouragement. Should there be someone at this period who happens to offend him in some way or other, this too the demon uses to contribute further to his hatred. This demon drives him along to desire other sites where he can more easily procure life's necessities, more readily find work and make a real success of himself. He goes on to suggest that, after all, it is not the place that is the basis of pleasing the Lord. God is to be adored everywhere. He joins to these reflections the memory of his dear ones and of his former way of life. He depicts life stretching out for a long period of time, and brings before the mind's eye the toil of the ascetic struggle and, as the saying has it, leaves no leaf unturned to induce the monk to forsake his cell and drop out of the fight. No other demon follows close upon the hells of this one (when he is defeated) but only a state of deep peace and inexpressible joy arise out of this struggle.[39]

Finally, as we learn from Evagrius, the best way to combat the demon of *acedia* is through the exercise of the virtue of hope implanted in us since our baptism (cf. Psalm 42:5–6). We must stand firm in the face of this noonday demon and wait upon the Lord's bidding because in this conflict the greatest purification of soul occurs. *Apatheia* and the love of God, self, and others in deep peace and harmony of soul flowers the moment this demon departs.

BEYOND SLOTH TO SERVICE

Remember those mornings when it's almost impossible to get up, dressed, and ready for work. Think of the litany of excuses that accompanies the demon of listlessness, and it is clear why his twin

---

39 Ibid., 12:18–19.

is the devil of dejection. A lazy, slothful, listless disposition slackens our fervor, makes procrastination attractive, and escalates our fears. We roam hither and yon, finding it impossible to commit ourselves to anything on a permanent basis. More often than not we find ourselves acting like "couch potatoes," indiscriminately watching TV with mouthfuls of junk food consumed during the commercials. We engage in empty chatter, never separated from our cell phone. We are like the monk who thinks

> he will not be able to rid himself of this grievous sickness, except by sallying forth frequently to visit his brethren, ostensibly to help them and to tend them if they are unwell. When he cannot lead him astray in this manner, [the demon of listlessness] puts him into the deepest sleep. In short, his attacks become stronger and more violent, and he cannot be beaten off except through prayer, through avoiding useless speech, through the study of the Holy Scripture and through patience in the face of temptation. If he finds a monk unprotected by these weapons, he strikes him down with his arrows, making him a wayward and lazy wanderer, who roams idly from monastery to monastery, thinking only of where he can get something to eat and drink. The mind of someone affected by listlessness is filled with nothing but vain distraction. Finally he is ensnared in worldly things and gradually becomes so grievously caught up in them that he abandons the monastic life altogether.[40]

Unruly, dissipated behavior accompanies the vice of listlessness. One is lax in reverence, impulsive in speech, quick to condemn, and unfit for stillness. The toxicity listless people spread around them rightly demands the tactic of avoidance. Like a plague laziness breeds more of the same. Work slacks off. Busybody gossip replaces sound conversation. Curiosity cancels study and the quest for truth. Quiet, steady production wanes. Taking advantage of others' generosity becomes second nature.

---

40 Cassian, *Philokalia*, 89.

According to the orthodox mystic St. Theophan the Recluse, "We grow cold within when our heart is distracted, when it cleaves to something other than God, worrying about different things, getting angry and blaming someone. . . . Guard against these things, and the coldness [listlessness] will diminish."[41]

Listless living erodes the motivation to pray unceasingly and to work diligently. Radically disobeyed is the Benedictine rule concerning *ora et labora*. Such a chronic lack of accomplishment is a breeding ground for low-grade depression. Overeating may be a symptom of seeking comfort food to compensate for a loss of meaning. Hyper-distraction replaces attentiveness and one's life becomes like a "walking coma."

The bad effects of sloth make it necessary to combat this demon by replacing an "I could care less" mentality by intentional and concerted care and concern. It helps if we develop realistic spiritual goals and try to realize them on a daily basis. The more aware we are of how this demon operates, the more we can diagnose the causes and effects of this evil and uproot it from our soul. As Cassian reminds us:

> The holy fathers of Egypt, who were brought up on the basis of these apostolic commandments, do not allow monks to be without work at any time, especially while they are young. They know that by persevering in work monks dispel listlessness, provide for their own sustenance and help those who are in need. They not only work for their own requirements, but from their labor they also minister to their guests, to the poor and to those in prison, believing that such charity is a holy sacrifice acceptable to God. The fathers also say that as a rule someone who works is attacked and afflicted by but a single demon, while someone who does not work is taken prisoner by a thousand evil spirits.[42]

This demon affects our capacity for diligent labor, but striving to subdue its vicious attacks is also necessary on the spiritual plane.

41 *The Art of Prayer: An Orthodox Anthology* (London: Faber & Faber, 1966), 257–261.
42 Cassian, *Philokalia*, 90.

According to St. John of the Cross, sloth causes souls to become weary in regard to their spiritual exercises and to flee from them, especially when they do not produce the sensory satisfactions one craves. The main cause of this listless response has to do with their chronic demands for more excitement, combined with their inability to be content with the common ways of deepening faith like liturgy, Word, and sacrament. They overlook the "richness of the ordinary" and become bored when they do not find excessive stimulation. In addition to boredom they begin to begrudge the small efforts it takes to serve God and others: "Because of their sloth, they subordinate the way of perfection (which requires denying one's own will and satisfaction for God) to the pleasure and delight of their own will."[43]

Sloth causes the soul to become increasingly averse towards adapting one's will to God's. One overlooks the key teaching of the Gospel that those who lose their life for God's sake will gain it and those who desire to gain it will lose it (cf. Matthew 16:25). This obstacle, which soon overtakes the person as a whole, blocks obedience to God's call to saintly, self-giving service and leads to the avoidance of any task that is routine, difficult, or unpleasant. In short, sloth is scandalized by the Cross and repelled by the "narrow gate" that leads to life (Matthew 7:13). It makes us extremely lax in fortitude and misses the labor spiritual maturity demands.

In the *Praktikos* Evagrius affirms the connection between *acedia* or dejection and *sloth* or listlessness. The latter vice manifests a "de-energizing" effect on the soul due to the deprivation of one's fantasy life and one's inordinate attachment to felt satisfaction. Sloth may lead to day dreaming about what it would take to make one happy and thereby curtail one's possibility of serving others where they are. One tends to "live in one's head," to waste time, and to feel dejected when little or nothing is accomplished. *The only cure for sloth is faithful service.*

---

43 John of the Cross, *The Dark Night*, 7:2, 374.

BEYOND GLUTTONY TO MODERATION

In a society replete with eating disorders, it is like a breath of fresh air to consider this ancient wisdom on what to eat, how much to consume, when to fast, and how to control one's consumption. Cassian does not offer blanket rules to cover everyone, but attends to each of us in our uniqueness. He cites the "Holy Fathers" like Evagrius, who stress that we have not been given only a single rule for fasting or a single standard and measure for eating. Everyone does not have the same strength. Age, illness, and bodily constitution account for these differences. The single goal we all share is to avoid over-eating and the temptation to gluttony. As Cassian says, fasting for one day can be of more benefit than rigorous plans to extend this ascetical practice over a number of days. He recommends common sense and moderation because

> someone who fasts for too long . . . often ends up by eating too much food. The result is that at times the body becomes enervated through undue lack of food and sluggish over its spiritual exercises, while at other times, weighed down by the mass of food it has eaten, it makes the soul listless and slack.[44]

Such teaching recognizes that dietary customs differ from person to person: "One man . . . could eat two pounds of dry bread and still be hungry, while another might eat a pound or only six ounces and be satisfied."[45] It is forbidden by the Fathers to gorge oneself. Gluttony is the sister vice of lust or unchastity; it plants in the soul the "seed of profligacy" and results in many sorts of self-indulgence. In short, "food is to be taken in so far as it supports our life, but not to the extent of enslaving us to the impulses of desire. To eat moderately and reasonably is to keep the body in health, not to deprive it of holiness."[46]

---

44 Cassian, *Philokalia*, 73.
45 Ibid., 73.
46 Ibid., 74.

Modern dieticians would agree with Cassian's "rule for self-control," which is this: "Stop eating while still hungry and do not continue until you are satisfied." He comes to the sensible conclusion that "by itself abstinence from food does not contribute to perfect purity of soul unless the other virtues are active as well." Here is a brilliant summary of his analysis:

> Humility, for example, practiced through obedience in our work and through bodily hardship, is a great help. If we avoid avarice not only by having no money, but also by not wanting to have any, this leads us towards purity of soul. Freedom from anger, from dejection, self-esteem and pride also contributes to purity of soul in general, while self-control and fasting are especially important for bringing about that specific purity of soul, which comes through restraint and moderation. Our initial struggle therefore must be to gain control of our stomach and to bring our body into subjection not only through fasting but also through vigils, labors and spiritual reading, and through concentrating our heart on fear of Gehenna and on longing for the kingdom of heaven.[47]

Turning to St. John of the Cross, we learn that spiritual gluttony causes us to focus inordinately on the tastes and touches of consolation we may initially experience when we do our spiritual exercises:

> Some attracted by the delight they feel in [these] exercises, kill themselves with penances, and others weaken themselves by fasts and, without the counsel or command of another, overtax their weakness; indeed, they try to hold these penances from one to whom they owe obedience in such matters. Some even dare perform these penances contrary to obedience.[48]

---

47 Ibid., 74.
48 John of the Cross, *The Dark Night*, 6:1, 371.

Briefly, gluttony means in this regard that we strive more for "spiritual savor" than for "spiritual purity and discretion."

We may also be inclined to go from one extreme to another, wavering between sacrifice and sensation without recognizing the risk of opening ourselves to demonic manipulation and the temptation to gratify our own will. This vice leads to loss of devotion and repugnance for the Cross; it blocks patient perseverance and makes us feel averse to any form of self-denial. It keeps us from making progress to a more mature spiritual life that seeks the mean between extremes and values moderation in all things. As St. John says: "Since all extremes are vicious and since by such behavior these persons are doing their own will, they grow in vice rather than in virtue. For through this conduct they at least become spiritually gluttonous and proud, since they do not tread the path of obedience."[49]

The greatest problem gluttony poses, in St. John's view, is that "spiritual gluttons" reach the point where the mere obligation of obedience in regard to spiritual exercises makes them lose all desire and devotion. "Their only yearning and satisfaction is to do what they feel inclined to do." And what happens if they do not get what they want. He replies without hesitation:

> They become sad and go about like testy children. They are under the impression that they do not serve God when they are not allowed to do what they want. Since they take gratification and their own will as their support and their god, they become sad, weak, and discouraged when their director takes these from them and desires that they do God's will. They think that gratifying and satisfying themselves is serving and satisfying God.[50]

The opposites of spiritual gluttony are sobriety and temperance. Inherent in the practice of self-denial is the need for moderation.

---

49 Ibid., 6:2, 371.
50 Ibid., 6:3, 372.

Otherwise, the temptation to mistake the taste and savor of the Lord for the Lord Himself may be too hard to resist.

> All their time is spent looking for satisfaction and spiritual consolation; they can never read enough spiritual books, and one minute they are meditating on one subject and the next on another, always hunting for some gratification in the things of God. God very rightly and discreetly and lovingly denies this satisfaction to beginners. If he did not, they would fall into innumerable evils because of their spiritual gluttony and craving for sweetness. This is why it is important for these beginners to enter the dark night and be purged of this childishness.[51]

Evagrius Ponticus says in the *Praktikos* that gluttony is first in the order of vices. As we learned in *The Dark Night*, it causes one to give up ascetic efforts *in short order*. "It brings to his mind concerns for his stomach, for his liver and spleen, the thought of a long illness, scarcity of the commodities of life and finally of his edematous [excessive accumulation of water] body and the lack of care by the physicians."[52] Finally, one blames one's gluttony on the ascetic life itself, thereby successfully twisting the truth that the only cure for gluttony is the wise discipline that accompanies moderation and puts to flight the demons who rule over the belly and other bodily passions.

BEYOND LUSTFUL LIVING TO CHASTE LOVING

The rise of infidelity in our culture is one indicator of the almost uncontrollable force of lust, which severs one from the discipline of chaste, respectful loving that is both responsible and open to the marital gift of procreation. The problem, succinctly put by Cassian, is that the "demon of unchastity and the desire of the flesh ... [begin] to trouble man from the time of his youth. This harsh struggle has to

---

51 Ibid., 6:6, 373.
52 Evagrius Ponticus, *The Praktikos*, 7:17.

be fought in both soul and body, and not simply in the soul, as is the case with other faults. We therefore have to fight it on two fronts."[53]

Bodily restraint in keeping with one's called, committed, and consecrated life has to be complimented by purity of heart. Otherwise, as Jesus said, a man can lust after a woman with his eyes and commit adultery without touching her (cf. Matthew 5:28). Such self-control, according to Cassian, "must be accompanied by contrition of heart, intense prayer to God, frequent meditation on the Scriptures, toil and manual labor. These are able to check the restless impulses of the soul and to recall it from its shameful fantasies."[54] Cassian places great store in humility of soul since [it] "helps more than everything else . . . and without it no one can overcome unchastity or any other sin."[55] That is why "we must take the utmost care to guard the heart from base thoughts, for, according to the Lord, 'out of the heart proceed evil thoughts, murders, adulteries, unchastity' and so on (Matthew 15:19)."[56]

Watchfulness is essential—from mortifying our thoughts to practicing modesty of the eyes. It is not enough to engage in bodily fasting. We must also pay attention to our thoughts and subdue their ramblings by spiritual meditation. Otherwise, we are not likely to advance to the heights of purity of heart and chaste, respectful love. The inside and the outside of our cup and plate both need to be clean (cf. Matthew 23:25). Such "a victory is beyond man's natural powers. . . . No one can soar to this high and heavenly prize of holiness on his own wings and learn to imitate the angels, unless the grace of God leads him upwards from this earthly mire."[57] Inquisitive and unchaste eyes lead us quickly down the wrong path. Cassian cites the Book of Proverbs, which does not say, "Keep your eyes with all diligence" but "Keep your heart with all diligence" (Proverbs 4:23). Cassian cites many passages from the Scriptures to prove that we cannot fully acquire the virtue of purity unless we have first acquired humility of

---

53 Cassian, *Philokalia,* 75.
54 Ibid., 75.
55 Ibid., 75.
56 Ibid., 75.
57 Ibid., 75–76.

heart. By the same token, we will not be granted the knowledge that comprises spiritual wisdom as long as the passion of unchastity lurks in the hidden depths of our souls.

This passage from vice to virtue benefits from one of the soundest of Cassian's counsels.

> We should therefore try to achieve not only bodily control, but also contrition of heart with frequent prayers of repentance, so that with the dew of the Holy Spirit we may extinguish the furnace of our flesh, kindled daily by the king of Babylon with the bellows of desire (Daniel 3:19). In addition, a great weapon has been given us in the form of sacred vigils, for just as the watch we keep over our thoughts by day brings us holiness at night, so vigil at night brings purity to the soul by day."[58]

These ancient counsels remain alive and active when we practice chaste respectful loving towards everyone in our circle of family and friends and especially when we pray for the grace to live chastely. Modesty in our appearance is another virtue that teaches, especially the young, how to live in respect for self and others. Adults need to set a good example and remain close to the Lord to replace the vice of lust with the virtue of love.

Even in the spiritual life itself, lust has its day. According to St. John of the Cross, it accommodates transcendent longings to sensate desires rather than lifting the senses chastely and respectfully to God. As he explains,

> The spirit, the superior part of the soul, experiences renewal and satisfaction in God; and the sense, the lower part, feels sensory gratification and delight because it is ignorant of how to get anything else, and hence takes whatever is nearest, which is the impure sensory satisfaction. It may happen that while a soul is with

---

58 Ibid., 77.

God in deep spiritual prayer, it will conversely passively experience sensual rebellions, movements, and acts in the senses, not without its own great displeasure.[59]

Lustful living in the spiritual realm opens us to the danger of demonic seduction; it arouses impure imaginations, a fantasy life replete with unrealistic expectations and unlawful remembrances. Of this danger St. John says,

> Through fear, some souls grow slack in their prayer—which is what the devil wants—in order to struggle against these movements, and others give it up entirely, for they think these feelings come while they are engaged in prayer rather than at other times. And this is true because the devil excites these feelings while souls are at prayer, instead of when they are engaged in other works, so that they might abandon prayer. And that is not all; to make them cowardly and afraid, he brings vividly to their minds foul and impure thoughts. And sometimes the thoughts will concern spiritually helpful things and persons. Those who attribute any importance to such thoughts, therefore, do not even dare look at anything or think about anything lest they thereupon stumble into them.[60]

This obstacle leads to remorse of conscience and can block our memory of God's mercy, especially if the origin of the lust is too much liking for another person, contrary to one's celibate or marital vocation. The purgation of spiritual lust occurs when we are granted the gift of sensory dryness, of aridity and distaste for anything but God whose grace leads us in the direction of chaste loving. A few of the benefits of this way of purifying formation, illuminating reformation, and unifying transformation are:

---

59 John of the Cross, *The Dark Night*, 4:2, 367.
60 Ibid., 4:3, 368.

- Practice of the virtues of faith, hope, and love; prudence, justice, fortitude, and temperance; of the corporal and spiritual works of mercy; and of the gifts and fruits of the Holy Spirit.
- The grace of habitual remembrance of God and a peace and joy that surpasses understanding.
- Unexpected touches, delights, and favors from God that occur suddenly, often in the midst of aridity.
- A newfound spirit, that is to say, a sense of being freed by God from the worldliness of the world, the prison of pretranscendent desires, the seductions of the demonic.
- Acting solely on the basis of love of God, neighbor, and self in God.
- Calming of the passions of gratification (joy), depression (sorrow), expectation (hope), and anxiety (fear) by harmonizing our sensate life with the operations of the transcendent. This turn-about leads slowly but surely to the experience that the "house" of our longing for anything less than God is now all "stilled," even though the spirits of fornication, blasphemy, and scrupulosity are like storms that flare up when least expected.

In conclusion, St. John says,

> Love, derived from sensuality terminates in sensuality; and the love that is of the spirit terminates in the spirit of God, and brings it increase. . . . When the soul enters the dark night, all these loves are placed in reasonable order. This night strengthens and purifies the love that is of God, and takes away and destroys the other."[61]

In the *Praktikos* Evagrius claims that the "demon of impurity" launches its most vicious attacks on those who exercise continence in

---

61 Ibid., 4:7–8, 370.

the single life and fidelity in marriage, in the hope that they will give up the practice of these virtues. The demon plays on the feeling that one may gain little or nothing from chaste loving—often exposing the soul to impure addictions, to defilements of the dignity of responsible and procreative love, and to the evocation of lustful images forbidden by Holy Scripture. Evagrius cautions us to remain vigilant, to halt these thoughts, and to pray for the grace to be more Christ-centered by maintaining continence and fidelity and by becoming more receptive to the grace of chaste, respectful love.

CONCLUSION

In conclusion, Cassian, John of the Cross, and Evagrius warn us that vice tightens its grip on our soul because it tempts us to go beyond moderation to one of the other forms of excess, for example, by making one live to eat rather than eating to live. The amount or quality of one's emotional response soars beyond what is requisite, for example, to show anger in the face of injustice but not to identify with the oppressor by resorting to violence. Superfluity, intemperance, and over-indulgence escalate the already extreme climate in which each of the seven capital sins thrives.

Their checkmate is moderation. It teaches us the art and discipline of operating within reasonable limits and thus preventing our actions from becoming excessive or violent or severe. Instead, our approach to life is regulated by virtues like patience and humility; it is controlled by putting others' needs, not our own, first; it is temperate and prone to operate in the mild climate of gentleness and equanimity.

Fortunately for us, Jesus taught by story and example how to go from enslavement to sin to the freedom of salvation. His whole purpose was to release us from the blinding effects of our fallenness. The good news is that these eight evil thoughts, and the seven capital sins they spawn, need not constitute our identity as human beings. We have received from birth a unique-communal call to service of God and neighbor, to generosity and patience, to modest habits of eating and dressing, to humility of mind and heart. The way of the Lord leads to release from the bondage of sin and the blinding fog of confusion in which it compels us to live. Goodness simply makes more sense than selfish, evil actions that harm more than help us and others. The choice is ours. May we, with God's help, make the right one.

REFERENCES

Anonymous. *The Cloud of Unknowing*. Edited by James Walsh, New York: Paulist Press, 1981.

Augustine, St. *Confessions*. Translated by John K. Ryan. Garden City, NY: Image Books, 1960.

Benedict, St. *The Rule of St. Benedict*. Edited by Abbot Justin McCann. London: Sheed & Ward, 1972.

Bennett, William J. *The Book of Virtues: A Treasury of Great Moral Stories*. New York: Simon & Schuster, 1993.

Bonhoeffer, Dietrich. *The Cost of Discipleship*. Translated by R. H. Fuller. New York: Touchstone, 1995.

Brother Lawrence of the Resurrection. *The Practice of the Presence of God*. Translated by Salvatore Sciuba. Washington, DC: ICS Publications, 1994.

Chesterton, G. K. *Orthodoxy*. Garden City, NY: Doubleday, 1959.

_____. *Heretics*. London: John Lane, 1952.

de Foucauld, Charles. *Hope in the Gospels*. New York: New City Press, 1990.

_____. *Meditations of a Hermit*. New York: Orbis Books, 1981.

_____. *The Way of the Christian Mystics*. Collegeville, MN: The Liturgical Press, 1990.

de Sales, St. Francis. *Introduction to the Devout Life*. Translated by John K. Ryan. New York: Image Books, Doubleday, 1972.

Hausherr, Irénée. *Penthos: The Doctrine of Compunction in the Christian East*. Translated by Anselm Hufstader. Kalamazoo, MI: Cistercian Publications. 1982.

John of the Cross, St. *The Collected Works*. Translated by Kieran Kavanaugh, O.C.D. and Otilio Rodriguez, O.C.D. Washington, DC: Institute of Carmelite Studies, 1991.

Julian of Norwich, *The Classics of Western Spirituality. Julian of Norwich: Showings*. Translated by Edmund Colledge and James Walsh. New York: Paulist Press, 1978.

Mother Teresa. *Come Be My Light: The Private Writings of the "St. of Calcutta."* Edited by Brian Kolodiejchuk, MC. New York: Doubleday, 2007.

Muto, Susan. *Blessings that Make Us Be: A Formative Approach to Living the Beatitudes*. Pittsburgh, PA: Epiphany Books, 2002.

_____. *Catholic Spirituality from A to Z: An Inspirational Dictionary*. Pittsburgh, Pennsylvania: Epiphany Books, 2005.

_____. *Keepsakes for the Journey: Four Weeks on Faith Deepening*. Hyde Park, NY: New City Press, 2010.

_____. *Meditation in Motion*. Pittsburgh, PA: Epiphany Books, 2001.

_____. *One in the Lord: Living Our Call to Christian Community*. Hyde Park, NY: New City Press, 2013.

_____. *Pathways of Spiritual Living*. Pittsburgh, PA: Epiphany Books, 2004.

_____. *A Practical Guide to Spiritual Reading*. Petersham, MA: St. Bede's Publications, 1994.

_____. *Words of Wisdom for Our World: The Precautions and Counsels of St. John of the Cross*. Eugene, OR: Wipf and Stock, 2009.

Muto, Susan and Adrian van Kaam. *The Commandments: Ten Ways to a Happy Life and a Healthy Soul*. Pittsburgh, PA: Epiphany Books, 1996.

_____and Adrian van Kaam. *Divine Guidance: Seeking to Find and Follow the Will of God*. Pittsburgh, PA: Epiphany Books, 2000.

_____and Adrian van Kaam. *Growing through the Stress of Ministry*. Williston Park, NY: Resurrection Press, 2005.

The Philokalia. 4 volumes. Translated and edited by G. E. H. Palmer, Philip Sherrard, Kallistos Ware. London: Faber and Faber, 1983, 1990, 1995, 1998.

Pieper, Josef. *A Brief Reader on the Virtues of the Human Heart*. San Francisco: Ignatius Press, 1991.

_____. *The Four Cardinal Virtues*. Notre Dame, IN: University of Notre Dame Press, 1966.

Teresa of Avila, St. *The Collected Works*. Volume 1, *The Book of Her Life*. Translated by Otilio Rodriguez and Kieran Kavanaugh. Washington, DC: Institute of Carmelite Studies, 1987.

_____. *The Collected Works*. Volume 2, *The Way of Perfection*. Translated by Otilio Rodriguez and Kieran Kavanaugh. Washington, DC: Institute of Carmelite Studies, 1980.

Theophan the Recluse. *The Spiritual Life and How to Be Attuned to It*. Translated by Alexandra Dockham. Forestville, CA: St. Herman of Alaska Brotherhood, 1996.

Thérèse of Lisieux, St. *Story of a Soul: The Autobiography of St. Thérèse of Lisieux*. Translated by John Clarke. Washington, DC: ICS Publications. 1975.

Thoreau, Henry David. *Walden*. Boston, MA: Houghton Mifflin, 1960.

van Kaam, Adrian. *Formative Spirituality Series*. Volume 3, *Formation of the Human Heart*. Pittsburgh, PA: Epiphany Books, 2002.

_____. *The Roots of Christian Joy*. Denville, NJ: Dimension Books, 1985.

_____. *Spirituality and the Gentle Life*. Pittsburgh, PA: Epiphany Books, 2005.

van Kaam, Adrian and Susan Muto. *Formation Theology Series*. Volume 3, *Formation of the Christian Heart*. Pittsburgh, PA: Epiphany Books, 2006.

_____. *The Power of Appreciation: A New Approach to Personal and Relational Healing*. Pittsburgh, PA: Epiphany Books, 1999.

Webb, Lance. *When Virtues Become Sins: God's Love and Human Transformation*. Nashville: Abingdon Press, 1959.

Wesley, John and Charles. *Selections from their Writings and Hymns*. Annotation by Paul Wesley Chilcote. Woodstock, VT: Skylight Paths, 2011.

_____. *Selected Writings and Hymns*. New York: Paulist Press, 1981.

ABOUT THE AUTHOR

Susan Muto, PhD, executive director of the Epiphany Association and a native of Pittsburgh, is a renowned speaker, author, teacher, and dean of the Epiphany Academy of Formative Spirituality. A single laywoman living her vocation in the world and doing full time, Church-related ministry in the Epiphany Association, she has led conferences, seminars, workshops, and institutes throughout the world.

Professor Muto received her PhD in English literature from the University of Pittsburgh, where she specialized in the work of post-Reformation spiritual writers. Beginning in 1966, she served in various administrative positions at the Institute of Formative Spirituality (IFS) at Duquesne University and taught as a full professor in its programs, edited its journals, and served as its director from 1981 to 1988. An expert in literature and spirituality, she continues to teach courses on an adjunct basis at many schools, seminaries, and centers of higher learning. She aims in her teaching to integrate the life of prayer and presence with professional ministry and in-depth formation in the home, the Church, and the marketplace.

As editor of the online publications *Epiphany Connexions, Epiphany Inspirations,* and *Epiphany International*, as a frequent contributor to scholarly and popular journals, and as the author and co-author with

Reverend Adrian van Kaam, CSSp, PhD (1920–2007) of more than forty books, Dr. Muto keeps up to date with the latest developments in her field. In fact, her many books on formative reading of Scripture and the masters are considered to be premiere introductions to the classical art and discipline of formative spirituality and its systematic, comprehensive formation science, anthropology, and theology. She lectures nationally and internationally on the treasured wisdom of the Judeo-Christian faith and formation tradition, and on many foundational facets of living human and Christian values and virtues in today's world.

Professor Muto holds membership in numerous honorary organizations and has received many distinctions for her work, including a Doctor of Humanities degree from King's College in Wilkes-Barre, Pennsylvania. She was also one of four Catholic writers to be honored in 2009 with a lifetime achievement award by the Catholic Historical Society of Western Pennsylvania. She is also the recipient of the 2014 Aggiornamento Award presented by the Parish and Community Library Services Section of the Catholic Library Association in recognition of an outstanding contribution made by an individual or an organization to the ministry of renewal modeled by Pope John XXIII (1881–1963). For more information on her life and ministry, go to www.epiphanyassociation.org or epiphanyacademyofformativespirituality.org.

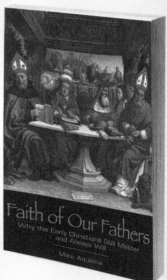

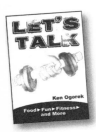

CATHOLIC FOR A REASON
Series

This benchmark series brings together the expert knowledge and personal insight of top Catholic apologists on topics at the heart of the Faith. A must-have for any Catholic's bookshelf.

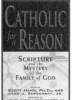

Catholic for a Reason
Scripture and the Mystery of the Family of God
Scott Hahn and Leon J. Suprenant, Jr., editors

Become a more articulate defender of the Faith. Join Jeff Cavins, Scott and Kimberly Hahn, and nine other well-known Catholic apologists for a heartfelt and deeply scriptural discussion on the Church as the family of God.

978-0-966322-30-9; 310 pages, $15.95, paperback

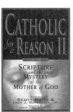

Catholic for a Reason II
Scripture and the Mystery of the Mother of God
Scott Hahn and Leon J. Suprenant, Jr., editors

Catholic teaching on Mary *is* scriptural. And in this moving tribute to Mary, nine Catholic authors, many of them converts, set out to explain exactly *why*. The second edition includes a new chapter on the Luminous Mysteries and an appendix on Marian dogmas.

978-1-931018-23-4; 227 pages, $15.95, paperback

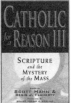

Catholic for a Reason III
Scripture and the Mystery of the Mass
Scott Hahn and Regis J. Flaherty, editors

Twelve outstanding Catholic authors examine the Mass in the context of the Old Testament, the early Church, the Apocalypse, evangelization, and Christian living. This dynamic and very readable book will increase your understanding and deepen your praying of the Mass.

978-1-931018-18-0; 203 pages, $15.95, paperback

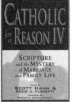

Catholic for a Reason IV
Scripture and the Mystery of Marriage and Family Life
Scott Hahn and Regis J. Flaherty, editors

Marriage and family life lived according to God's plan can change lives and change the world! This book explores the scriptural basis for the Catholic understanding of marriage. Join twelve well-known Catholic authors, who along with their spouses, present solid biblical testimony to the joys, struggles, and sanctity found in the Sacrament of Marriage.

978-1-931018-44-9; 224 pages, $15.95, paperback

Emmaus Road Publishing • emmausroad.org

find out why

real men choose

VIRTUE

N eed a spiritual workout? *Boys to Men: The Transforming Power of Virtue*, by Tim Gray and Curtis Martin, is a Bible study designed specifically for men who want to build their spiritual strength. Each chapter focuses on a different virtue necessary to help raise a new generation of godly men. With challenging questions at the end of each chapter, this book is ideal for individual or group study. Find out why real men choose the virtuous life!

Boys to Men may be ordered directly through Emmaus Road Publishing for only $11.95 (plus shipping and handling), or by visiting your local Catholic bookstore.